homesick

nomad

Also by Brianna Madia

Nowhere for Very Long

Never Leave the Dogs Behind

homesick nomad

SETTLING INTO AN UNTETHERED LIFE

brianna madia

HarperOne
An Imprint of HarperCollinsPublishers

Without limiting the exclusive rights of any author, contributor or the publisher of this publication, any unauthorized use of this publication to train generative artificial intelligence (AI) technologies is expressly prohibited. HarperCollins also exercise their rights under Article 4(3) of the Digital Single Market Directive 2019/790 and expressly reserve this publication from the text and data mining exception.

HOMESICK NOMAD. Copyright © 2026 by Brianna Madia. All rights reserved. No part of this book may be used or reproduced in any manner whatsoever without written permission except in the case of brief quotations embodied in critical articles and reviews. For information, address HarperCollins Publishers, 195 Broadway, New York, NY 10007. In Europe, HarperCollins Publishers, Macken House, 39/40 Mayor Street Upper, Dublin 1, D01 C9W8, Ireland.

HarperCollins books may be purchased for educational, business, or sales promotional use. For information, please email the Special Markets Department at SPsales@harpercollins.com.

hc.com

FIRST EDITION

Designed by Jason Kayser

Library of Congress Cataloging-in-Publication Data has been applied for.

ISBN 978-0-06-344013-5

Printed in the United States of America

26 27 28 29 30 LBC 5 4 3 2 1

To William
for the penny, the clover, and the ring

AUTHOR'S NOTE

As always, my stories are told to the best of my memory. (If I hadn't lived through some of the events in this book, I may not believe them myself.)

And while some names have been changed and last names omitted, it is not for protection. It's for closure. Their story is done impeding on mine. But we all know the internet is forever.

The only truth is that I live.
Sincerely, I live.
Who am I?
Well, that's a bit much.

—CLARICE LISPECTOR

CONTENTS

chapter one	The Wrong Girl	1
chapter two	What Did You Expect?	16
chapter three	Never Leave the Dogs Behind	35
chapter four	My Beach	42
chapter five	Dirt Road Etiquette	61
chapter six	The Taco Truck	69
chapter seven	Trailer for Two	80
chapter eight	Where To	97
chapter nine	Back to Bend	108
chapter ten	What's Yours Is Yours	126
chapter eleven	The Science of Packing	131
chapter twelve	You'll Change Your Mind	142
chapter thirteen	Mom	154
chapter fourteen	Twenty-Four Hours on the Low Road	164
chapter fifteen	Exit 241	190
chapter sixteen	Gone. Missing.	195
chapter seventeen	Bertha	210
	Acknowledgments	223

homesick

nomad

chapter one

The Wrong Girl

I never said, "I want to be alone." I only said, "I want to be let alone." There is all the difference.

—GRETA GARBO

"If you're looking for someone to fall asleep next to every night, you've got the wrong girl..."

Those were the exact words I said back in 2020 to some well-meaning man, gazing at me from my passenger seat. We'd been sleeping together on and off for a few months. He claimed he was in love with me. He said he wished I didn't go off alone with the dogs so much. He said he wanted me to stay at his house in town.

"You don't even have air-conditioning in your trailer," he'd whine. "You'd be more comfortable at my place."

And where some folks might have fawned over a person so eager to take care of them, I couldn't get away fast enough. It made my skin crawl. In fact, the moment I hung up the phone after breaking it off, I jumped in my Jeep and drove sixty-eight miles out into the desert to sleep beside the Dirty Devil River, to wash the idea of ever trusting someone again right down into the muddy water.

For how unconventional just about everything in my life had turned out, the relationship aspect of it had been positively Americana. Neil and I met as kids, got together as teens, and married in our early twenties. If not for our total lack of religion and children, any preacher would have approved.

Having been with one person my whole life was this traditional piece that didn't always feel like it fit into the rest of the puzzle. In fact, it surprises a lot of folks when I say I was with someone for eleven years. Nowadays, I seem a touch too feral to believe that had ever been the case.

We never lived like a "proper" married couple, however. We crammed four people into studio apartments, rented houses with six of our closest friends. We lived like college kids until we were almost thirty. As a huge proponent of never growing up, I loved everything about it.

The only time Neil and I truly lived alone was one summer on a sailboat back in our early twenties, and then again when we moved into a big, orange, constantly breaking van named Bertha in 2017. We were so fixated on figuring out every intricate aspect of the life we had chosen that I don't think we had time to notice that we were growing apart.

It's hard to focus on tiny grievances when your main priority is trying to keep your home off of various tow trucks across the American Southwest, and watching your bank account drop with every click of the odometer. We saved up for tow truck fees the way folks save for their kid's college fund.

But tiny grievances add up. They fester.

In late 2019, we were renting a house with friends in Salt Lake City after one too many Bertha breakdowns. We finally had the space and the silence and the monotony of routine to realize that our marriage was about as broken as that van was.

It felt like pressing a scalpel to skin, cutting it open to reveal an infection that had spread beyond repair. And I didn't want to stay sick.

When I left him in the spring of 2020, I was in the position to "start over" in just about every sense of the word. I had printed out some bare-bones uncontested divorce paperwork from the Utah government's website.

We split what little money we had right down the middle. We had no kids to fight over. I didn't have an office job I'd have to quit. We didn't have a house to sell or even furniture that had cost enough to be worth the hassle of taking. The friends we'd been renting the place with were more than happy to keep the thrift store couch.

All I had to do was load my three dogs, my two pythons, and

a few boxes of clothes up into Bertha and drive away. All tethers to anything beyond that were severed by the final slamming of the front door.

I could have moved anywhere, been anything, deleted my *very* public Instagram account, changed my name, joined the circus, invented an entirely new life so as to forget about the one I was leaving behind. But there were parts of my life I *didn't* want to leave behind.

There were dreams that Neil and I had dreamt together, like owning our own land in the desert. But those dreams were just as much *mine* as they were ever *ours*.

With eyes still swollen, cheeks still salted with tears, I took a deep breath, clutched Bertha's wheel, and steered us southeast toward the little desert town of Moab to start over.

Or, as I see it now . . . to keep going.

By the fall of that same year, I had cashed out my retirement, sold my car, and used every last penny I had on a down payment for a loan to buy nine acres of desert out on a mesa south of town. It might have been *our* dream, but I and I alone had made it *my* reality.

Due to the Covid pandemic, loan companies were hesitant to dole out money, especially for a completely undeveloped plot of land. What would they do if I missed payments? Repossess some dirt in the middle of nowhere, Utah?

Miraculously, I found one company out of Rochester, New York, who said they'd give me the loan if I could put 50 percent down in cash, which equated to sixty-five thousand dollars. So, I quite literally gave them everything I had.

I'm sure they were shocked when I agreed to the terms, which included an interest rate of 14 percent and a deadline to pay it off within two years.

Was it the smartest thing to do? Probably not. But there's no rule that says all of your decisions have to be smart. In fact, the ones that seem kinda crazy are usually the ones that *really* change your life. Even more so if you make them on a whim, like I tend to do.

I wish I could tell you that accomplishing this dream made everything hurt less, but I still spent months up on that mesa absolutely blinded with grief, despite how surreally beautiful it all was.

After I secured the loan, I lived paycheck to paycheck. And while that's certainly not remarkable, it was especially nerve-racking not knowing when the next paycheck would come. (The woes of freelance work.)

I saved up enough to buy a twenty-two-foot, 1982 travel trailer, which I dragged up there after I had a long, winding dirt driveway put in. Night after night, I'd watch the sun disappear, casting neon pink across the easternmost wall of rocks that held my land in the crook of its arm.

Then I'd sit by candlelight until I successfully cried or drank myself to sleep.

I can't tell you exactly when it happened, because healing doesn't work like that. But after all those debilitating months of mourning what my life had been, I started to *really* fall in love with the idea of what my life could be . . . what I could do now that I had nothing but a car full of dogs, endless roads to choose from, and a piece of land in my name.

I'd leave my property in the morning after waking up whenever I damn well pleased, toss my empty coffee mug into the sink full of other empty coffee mugs, load the dogs up into the Jeep, and disappear for hours between winding canyons. I had no one to report to, nowhere to be, and nothing left to lose. I might as well have been factory reset.

Each night, I'd go home and eat cold noodles on the deck while the dogs rambled around between the two-hundred-year-old junipers. On average, juniper trees grow ten to fifteen centimeters a *year*, and that's if they survive the brutal flash floods that the desert is known for.

The one that Dagwood could almost *always* be found asleep beneath was over twelve feet tall. And that wasn't even the tallest. They enveloped us in every direction, so much so that from out on the dirt road, passersby couldn't see us at all. To be surrounded by that kind of quiet resilience was never lost on me.

Tears still came to me often, but they had become ones of gratitude. I'd cry watching my dogs running wild day after day in a desert we could call our own. I'd cry watching them fall asleep afterward in a great big pile on our very small bed.

I'd cry during sunsets and sunrises, full moons and new moons when it's so clear and so dark that you can see right through the Milky Way into other universes glowing in ethereal blues and greens like Arctic lights.

I had nothing but time to sit out there in all that stillness and figure out who I was.

I had always been independent, but this was an entirely new level of liberation. Almost everything I did, I did because it seemed to occur to me, only now, that I *could*.

For the first time in my life, I belonged only to myself. (And to my dogs, of course.)

By the spring of 2021, I had four of them. I'd subtracted one husband and doubled my dogs. A top-notch equation, if you ask me. Even better when you add in the two pythons, Bean and Mae.

Slowly acquiring my own small zoo felt like my second act of... radical free will, let's call it. Going for broke on land out in a place most people consider "nowhere" was most certainly the first. So after that, I decided almost any seemingly crazy idea might be worth trying.

I would make my life as ridiculous and eccentric and as full of failures as I pleased, because, all things considered, my failures had worked out pretty well for me. They chewed me up and spat me out right into a life that was uniquely and unmistakably *mine*.

And being unique and unmistakable has always been important to me. I don't recall a time in my life that I wanted to be like anyone (let alone everyone) else. I don't remember when the compulsion began, because it's been there for as long as all of my memories have. I used to spend a lot of time analyzing it, dissecting it to try to narrow down which particular childhood trauma caused this desperate need for individuality and approval (which is an *extremely* complicated combination, by the way).

But my mother reminded me of this often. "Brianna," she'd say, "you have *always* been this way. You have *always* been who you are. Long before your dad left. Long before you were even old enough to be aware of it."

Folks call me "eccentric" and "free-spirited" now, which in grade school translated to "weird."

I used to run around on all fours at recess, pretending I was a dog. If I wasn't doing that, I was wading through the waist-deep golden grasses on the far end of the field, collecting ladybugs in my special bug carrier.

One of my favorite pastimes was Rollerblading through the neighborhood with a python around my neck. For the majority of my childhood, I traveled almost exclusively on Rollerblades, including across the linoleum kitchen floor to get snacks (when my mom was at work, of course, because that was explicitly forbidden).

One of my snakes, Bean, was a dead ringer for the one my brother and I had as kids. His name was Zeus, and I can guarantee you that my brother and I argued over that. I'd take him gently from his tank in the basement, wrap his cold-blooded body around my warm neck, and Rollerblade around the neighborhood. Odd, for sure, but anything's better than boring.

A few weeks after I moved to Moab, I took Bean from his tank, laced up my "blades"—as all the cool kids called them—and queued up a Best-Disco-Songs-of-All-Time playlist.

I was pleasantly surprised with how easily the muscle memory returned, despite it being almost fifteen years since I'd done this. After only the first few hundred feet, Bean slowly extended his little head straight out into the wind as if he were a hood ornament on one of the Jaguars my friends' parents drove back in Connecticut. Zeus used to do the exact same thing.

Besides being the resident reptile nerd as a child, I was also a very dedicated performer. The door to our attic was in my bedroom closet, so it's more aptly considered an extension of my room.

Before a big show, I'd climb up the very steep, ever-so-slightly tilting steps and dig through my box of costumes. To this day, I can close my eyes and feel the carpet beneath my knees; smell the muggy summer heat saturating the wooden A-shaped ceiling.

After several minutes of rummaging, I would materialize in the living room dressed in velvet and top hats and feather boas and those little plastic glittery shoes all the girls had in the 1990s.

I'd teeter into the room, where my mother would erupt in applause at whatever interpretive dance routine I had come up with. (Enya was my go-to.) I always did some little performance when we had people over, but most of the time, it was only my mother who was privy to them. After all, most were just rehearsals for the holidays (busy season, lots of houseguests).

After taking my final bow, I'd make my way into the garage to gather my little mesh carrier for frogs and salamanders. Often, I'd swap out one of my fancy costume hats for one of my brother's baseball caps so I could bring along my five parakeets, who all loved to sit on top of my head. But parakeets are frequent poopers, so I always made sure it was onto my brother's hat instead of mine.

I usually left the birds at home when I walked down to the end of the street to feed the even bigger birds: a flock of geese that had become accustomed to my daily arrival with bread crusts and oyster crackers.

For that excursion, I'd bring along one of my pet rats instead. I had a special "rat jacket" because they are *also* frequent poopers. It was a soft old sweatshirt with two zip-up side pockets that I could adjust perfectly so their furry little noses and round pink ears could peek out.

I was asked several times by the owners of the neighborhood market to stop bringing rodents into their establishment, so visiting with the geese was a better activity for them.

When not being shooed out of local stores, I could be found cruising the waterfront on my blades with Zeus around my neck; my childhood dog, Lola, trotting along diligently behind me.

Kids at school teased me and the neighbors looked at me a little funny, but they also referred to me as Dr. Dolittle, which was the greatest compliment in the world to a girl who really believed she could talk to animals.

Although, this is something I've never grown out of.

By the age of thirty, I had swapped the glittery plastic heels for cowboy boots, but I was still always dressed up, covered in dirt, and surrounded by animals. My childhood routines, regardless of how strange they had been, became the foundation for my new ones. They were grounding, in a way.

Besides the snakes and my four dogs, Bucket, Dagwood, Birdie, and Banjo, there were often entire litters of puppies I'd foster from the local animal shelter. Sometimes it was a litter of four, sometimes eight. Nine was the most I ever had at once. Mind you, all these dogs and I were living out of a twenty-two-foot trailer that had no running water, no working toilet, and no temperature control.

I saying living "out of" a trailer instead of living "in" because most of our days were spent on the porch or wandering between the huge sandstone boulders and barrel cacti that dotted our nine acres. In the hotter months, we didn't have a choice. By noon, the inside of that metal trailer was a sweat lodge. It got so hot in there, it actually melted my makeup. I unzipped the pouch one afternoon to what looked like an abstract oil painting.

I affectionately referred to my property as Puppy Preschool. I didn't teach them how to sit or stay, and I *certainly* never made them practice walking politely on a leash because none of mine even know how to do that. I thought of it more as showing them all the best things about being a dog.

They would roll in the dirt, wrestle with their siblings, hold their own in a battle of tug-of-war with Birdie, who was nearly three times their size. We'd search for muddy puddles and tracks of lizards' tails through the sand. They padded their tiny paws along behind me, right on my heels for each step I took.

I'd lie on the ground, drowning in puppies, as they clambered over me. The tiny scratches all across my legs, arms, and face didn't bother me. Neither did the exorbitant amount I had to spend on cleaning supplies for lots and lots of tiny bladders.

The very first litter of puppies I ever fostered were just seven-and-a-half-weeks old. Banjo, my youngest dog, was one of them. Over the years, he seemed to treat each new litter as a way to pay it forward: playing with them, nosing their little faces, leading them off to explore rocks and bushes they might have otherwise been too scared to. He wasn't unlike Nana from Peter Pan.

Which is fitting, given that Peter Pan may as well have been my life coach.

Each evening or afternoon or whenever I felt like it, I'd dig through my closet (which is still best described as a "box of costumes") to find something to wear to stroll the grounds.

In the early summer of 2021, I was fostering a litter of nine, so as I took off down the driveway, I had *thirteen* dogs in tow.

Given that the puppies were still so little, we'd usually only make it down to the end of the driveway and back. It was longer than a football field, after all.

When my dirt met the dirt road, I sat on a rock and watched as the all-black puppies sprawled out across the ground like an oil spill.

That's when I heard the car coming.

The mouth of the dirt road I live on is gated, so the occasional passersby were always assumed to be the neighbors that I never bothered to meet, as I'd taken to being a well-dressed, wild-eyed recluse.

I held my breath and started hurriedly ushering the sea of creatures back up toward the trailer, hoping they would just pass by. But I heard the crackling of gravel beneath the tires as a woman in a Subaru slowed to a stop; her incredulous face appearing slowly behind the lowering window.

I suppose I couldn't blame her, given that I was standing there in an ankle length, multitiered dress with bananas printed all over it, holding a glass of wine in one hand while Bean coiled himself around my other like a living bracelet. Around my neck was the massive turquoise squash blossom I'd bought from a fifth-generation Diné silversmith in New Mexico. Intertwined with the necklace was my other, larger python, Mae, who was the same color as the bananas on my dress.

And, of course, the thirteen dogs scattered around me in the driveway. I could see her trying to count them as I stood perfectly still, smiling awkwardly.

"What's the occasion?" she shouted over the eruption of barking dogs. Her face had gone from shock to visible amusement.

I smiled, shrugged, and shouted back over the car's idling engine, "All the world's a stage!"

There is a documentary from 1975 called *Grey Gardens* about the everyday lives of a reclusive mother and daughter who were living in a mansion that had fallen into a state of total disrepair. It had no running water and a noteworthy number of raccoons living in the walls. There were also fifty-two different cats roaming the property freely with odd names like Pinky One, Pinky Two, Little Jimmy, and Hipperino.

Despite the relative squalor they lived in, the duo strolled the grounds in elaborate outfits with scarves and jewels and furs from the days when they had exorbitant wealth. They were relatives of the Kennedy family by marriage, but were now what some might call high society dropouts.

The city had given them orders to fix the place up or face demolition, but that hadn't seemed to faze them. They just continued meandering around, singing opera songs from atop the dining room table or tap-dancing in the echo of the crumbling halls, rife with mangy cats who would climb in and out of various broken windows.

Nobody could really understand *why* they lived that way or how it had even gotten that way in the first place. Of course, there were speculations of mental illness (even back in the '70s, society rushed to assume that there was something deeply wrong with any person they couldn't quite understand).

But whether they had ever received any concrete diagnosis or not didn't interest me. I have a few diagnoses of my own, after all.

When I watched the movie for the first time in my early twenties, I thought they were some of the strangest, freest, most unabashed women I'd ever seen. They were the definition of not giving a damn what "normal" people thought of them, and they *certainly* didn't want to live the way those people thought they should.

After the first few months hiding out on my own somewhat

dilapidated property in my finest clothes and jewels with a sea of animals on my heels, I was finally starting to feel the same.

I'm sure I looked successful on paper by the age of thirty. I had bought my own land, finished my first book, and was what was considered "famous" on Instagram.

But by any suburban standard, I was *way* off track. Divorced, childless, living alone in the desert inside a trailer, having one-sided conversations with dozens of dogs. Regardless, being a complicated, somewhat unhinged woman out in the middle of nowhere really *did* feel like success to me.

I have always believed the best way to get what you want in this life is to start with what you don't. It's a shorter list, and a much more honest one.

Plus, there could be something out there that I haven't even thought to want yet, so I don't see the point in trying to count all the stars. First, I focus on the big black holes I don't want to get sucked into. I scarcely think about *exactly* where my ship is headed, so long as it is away from the kind of cookie-cutter life I'd witnessed growing up.

Those so-called normal milestones just never had my name on them. I've never wanted the big house and the picket fence, the rich husband, the country club membership, or the minivan full of kids. I refused to look up from that checklist one day and wonder where my life went. If that makes me the wrong kind of girl, well, then I'm exactly who I set out to be.

chapter two

What Did You Expect?

It's a question I hear all the time, especially since my divorce. "You're famous on Instagram because *you* put yourself out there... so what did you expect?"

It's amazing how easily it rolls off of people's tongues, as if they've never paused to consider what they're actually asking me. Didn't you *expect* people to be cruel?

If you really want to know what I "expected" from social media, I suppose I'd have to start at the beginning. All the way back in 2012, when a twenty-two-year-old girl living on an old sailboat in Bridgeport, Connecticut, downloaded an app called Instagram.

It was all the rage, and the first real photo-based social media site besides Facebook, which a lot of younger folks seemed disillusioned by. Suddenly our feeds were covered in news articles and randomly suggested videos and our grandmas reposting fake viral disclaimers telling Mark Zuckerberg that he didn't have permission to use their photos. It just wasn't hip anymore.

Instagram felt like a combination of Facebook and Twitter. A photograph with a few sentences beneath it. Most of the photos I posted in the beginning had no captions at all. In fact, they were mostly just different colored filters on Bucket's face. (She was only a year old at the time.)

I followed a couple dozen friends from high school and college, and that's about it. My feed was just grainy cell phone pictures of someone's pretty unremarkable dinner plate or a photo of a lamp that looked more artistic in black-and-white. It was a pretty mellow place.

I started posting photos on Instagram much more in 2014. Because, at the tender young age of twenty-four, I had already achieved what I was told was the most important thing a young lady could do. I got *married*. And I had the pictures to prove it.

Neil and I tied the knot barefoot on a grassy hillside under a big white tent where every inch of table surface was covered in mason jars and tealights and hydrangeas. Bucket wore pink, Dagwood had a bow tie, Neil had a man-bun, and I had a flower crown on my head the size of a front door wreath.

It was essentially a 2014 Pinterest wedding board come to life, so it wasn't too terribly surprising that a month or so after I received the photos, my photographer texted me excitedly saying that the Knot (a *huge* company widely considered the most trusted authority in wedding planning) wanted to do a feature about our wedding.

She was ecstatic. It was a *big* deal for a photographer to have their work on the Knot's website, as well as their social media.

There was one caveat, though. The Knot only shares wedding photos on Instagram from brides or grooms with *public* accounts. Basically, they want their followers to see one photo of your dress and be able to click on your profile to binge thirty-five more if they so desire, as opposed to having to individually answer 174 comments on their own page saying "Where is this dress from?!"

I looked up how to change my account from private to public, and after a few clicks, I texted my photographer to tell her it was done. Two weeks later, when the Knot posted the photos, over two thousand strangers started following me on Instagram.

I stared, dumbfounded, as the numbers rose and rose each time I opened the app. I wasn't sure what anyone would find overtly interesting about my life at that point. I was still largely posting photos of my (now two) dogs with emojis for captions, but folks seemed to stick around. The fact that they were strangers made me somehow *less* afraid to share my writing with them. I'm an extremely unserious person in real life, so I always felt like the people who really knew me might laugh at all these deeply introspective things I had to say.

Granted, the writing I was sharing was only the occasional paragraph-long caption. It felt a bit like a public diary. But people started to comment more regularly. People started to tell me I was a great writer.

About two and a half years after making my Instagram account public, outdoor retail giant REI reposted a photo of Bertha to their over one million followers. In that photo, Neil, Bucket, Dagwood, and I are all sitting and smiling in front of a behemoth orange Bertha out in the sunbaked, red-rocked desert outside Zion National Park with backpacks and climbing gear scattered everywhere. A dirtbag's dream.

Beyond being absolutely massive and the color of a traffic cone, Bertha was also as old as I was, which, at the time, was twenty-six years. She was originally used as a shuttle vehicle for a white-water rafting company in Colorado back in the '90s. The guys there swapped the axle out and did their own version of a 4WD conversion with parts from various 1970s F-150 pickup trucks.

They only needed her to be able to make it down one rocky slope at the river takeout. (I've taken her down many "rocky slopes" since the '90s, which is likely why she's broken all the time.)

Despite the mechanical woes we'd been dealing with since the very day we exchanged $7,800 for her in a warehouse parking lot north of Salt Lake, I was completely enamored with her. She was, without question, unique and unmistakable. I shouldn't have been as surprised as I was when that REI post got as much attention as it did.

Over the next forty-eight hours, twelve thousand more people started following me. It was incredibly overwhelming, but it was also so *cool* to think that all these people . . . cared? Thought living in an old van was an amazing idea?! Agreed that running around in the desert with your dogs was most certainly the meaning of life??

It would be like thousands of people just showing up on your daily jogging route one morning to cheer you on. In the beginning, it really was amazing. But these were still strangers. They didn't know our backstory.

The truth is, this is the only reason I started *really* writing on

Instagram. People asking about my story was the perfect reason to start telling it. To get *good* at telling it.

My captions became more introspective, more vulnerable. I wrote about how Neil and I had found each other, found Bucket, found Utah, found Dagwood, found Bertha. I wrote about sleeping in slot canyons at night with only a sliver of sky to tell the time. I wrote about the coyote calls at dusk, the hiss of heat from an old engine, the sun-faded blue jeans of the boy I loved. I wrote about the way the mesas and spires jut up across the desert horizon like a heartbeat on a monitor. I wrote about what it means to love a dog... what life could look like if you let both them *and you* run a little bit wild.

At the time of that REI post, we were living in Bertha full-time, but I was still working as a technical writer for a software company. Mind you, the term *influencer* didn't exist yet, let alone the idea that you could make a *living* off of social media.

I shared all of those pictures and stories just because I wanted to, just because it was a nice change from the mind-numbing user manuals I wrote at work. But they hadn't gone unnoticed by the masses, so companies started to take a stab at what is *now* the two-and-a-half-billion-dollar social media marketing industry.

My first "gig" was with a dog treat company. They asked if they could send me a box of treats *and* offered to reimburse me for gas to take photos of the adventures I took my dogs on every weekend anyway. I was ecstatic. (Bucket and Dagwood were too, obviously, but they always were.)

I have an exceptionally vivid memory of leaving my office building that Friday, driving south toward the desert. The windows were down, as they almost always were in Bertha, so I shouted over to Neil.

"Imagine if we could get free gas every weekend?!"

New followers continued to trickle in as the concept of "vanlife" swept the internet. But in 2017, a media group called the Dodo shared a video of Bucket and Dagwood to their millions of online followers. It was titled "Do These Dogs Have the Best Life in the World?" (I loudly remind Bucket of this when she is complaining about not being served dinner at 3:45 p.m.)

Over the next few weeks, that video amassed me over seventy thousand followers. Meaning at this point, I had almost one hundred thousand people watching me every day. The excitement was still palpable, but I distinctly remember feeling as though I was no longer in the driver's seat.

I woke up one morning, shocked to read a comment from a new follower saying they had read an article about me in the *Daily Mail*, which is a hugely popular British tabloid. I frantically scrolled through it, reading every word with my breath held. No one had interviewed me for this or called for a quote or asked permission in any way. I guess I had officially become "a public figure," meaning there was no obligation to do so.

Fortunately, the article was essentially just a description of my Instagram page. *Can you believe these people live in a big orange van? Click here to watch them rappel into slot canyons with their dogs! Look at how beautiful and whimsical it all is!*

I sat back from my laptop in my office and smiled. Bucket and Dagwood were asleep beneath my desk chair when I leaned down to tell them that they were famous in the UK. They blinked at me several times before closing their eyes again. They knew to sleep most of the day so that when five o'clock rolled around, they'd be ready to devolve back into the wild things we all were.

I leaned back in toward my screen and clicked to open the comment section beneath the article. This would be the first time I would make this mistake, but most certainly not the last.

I was surprised to find that the majority of people were positively incensed by the information they had just taken in. One guy said that I looked like Owen Wilson (which is now a long-running joke in my family), but the rest were more fixated on how I was *able* to just go live in a van and run around out in the desert. The broadly agreed-upon consensus was that I must have a trust fund.

My first thought, of course, was *What trust fund kid chooses to live in a rusted, old, consistently breaking-down van with no running water and a hole in the dirt for a toilet?* What exactly about my life was screaming exorbitant inherited wealth?

Strangers saying that I looked like Owen Wilson was funny, easy to shrug off. (I think he's quite handsome, to be honest.) But strangers assuming that I was some spoiled rich kid sent me over the edge.

It never helped when some of these articles or blog posts included the fact that I grew up in *Connecticut*. The name alone conjures images of old money and decadent mansions with pristine front lawns pruned by truckloads of Mexicans that come over the city line from Bridgeport. That's where I lived.

homesick nomad

. . .

The house I grew up in sat almost precisely on the line between the city of Bridgeport and the town of Fairfield. Fairfield is one of the wealthiest areas in the country, pressed flush up against Bridgeport, where more than 22 percent of the population lives below the poverty line. The distance between these two places is minuscule, but they might as well have been different worlds.

Bridgeport was rife with gang activity, drive-by shootings, and petty crime. To this day, I still forget to lock my car because I grew up knowing that it was better to leave it unlocked so would-be thieves could just open the door to find nothing of value, as opposed to smashing a window and *then* finding nothing of value.

Regardless, our neighborhood was quaint and had lots of young families. I liked where I lived. It was other people who made it seem like something I should be ashamed of. Even my own mother. She hated our zip code. She had us write *Fairfield* on any form of paperwork instead of *Bridgeport*. She wanted to live on the other side of that invisible but palpable line, but my dad was a carpenter and she was a school secretary. Safe to say it was out of budget.

The budget was reserved for sending my brother and me to private Catholic schools in different towns. The public schools in Bridgeport had metal detectors at every entrance, which used to be really unusual, despite being something Americans now widely, and depressingly, regard as normal.

My all-girls private Catholic school had no metal detectors and was chock-full of sixteen-year-olds with BMWs and maids who cleaned their rooms for them while their mothers played tennis.

In the evenings, fathers would shuffle home from their jobs in New York City, dull-eyed and often too exhausted to pay attention to a wife *or* kids. They were busy working themselves to the bone to afford a mansion with intercoms in each room because the house was too big for anyone to know that dinner was ready otherwise. There were entire rooms, entire "wings" that went untouched. I once asked a friend if anyone had ever sat in what was referred to as "the sitting room."

"Probably not," she said with a flippant laugh.

This, supposedly, was "the dream." Go to college (an Ivy League school *obviously*), get a job, get married, have kids, buy a big house and a bunch of nice cars and expensive crap for your "sitting room," then work until you're old enough to retire and just hope you've still got the energy and wherewithal to get started on that bucket list. People live their lives with such astounding, unfounded certainty. They assume their own tomorrows. They assume they're guaranteed to come.

All this to say, I grew up around kids who really *did* have trust funds, or parents who just handed them their own credit cards, the keys to their own Mercedes. And I had been reminded at almost every turn that I did *not*. And that made me different . . . worse, somehow. So, for a long time, I held a very sharp opinion about rich people. The last thing I wanted was to be accused of being one. It detracted from the rebellion that was the driving force behind what my life had become.

It was also infuriatingly ironic to think that I had fled from that *very* world in order to become the person these folks read that *very* article about.

I learned quickly that jealousy often begets cruelty. Though understanding that doesn't necessarily make it hurt less. But I also learned that when you do something enviably unusual, it's easier for people to believe you've "cheated" in some way, that you had some sort of loophole or shortcut. You must have family money or you're "living off assistance programs with *our* tax dollars!!!!" (I got that one a lot too.)

The reality is, this is a self-soothing mechanism for people; something to comfort them from the looming thought that maybe *they* could have done something different with their own lives. Maybe the dream they wrote off years ago could have been their reality if they'd been willing to brave the discomfort and the criticisms.

There is really only one thing that separates the naysayers in the comment sections from the folks they're commenting about. We tried. We leapt. That's always within reach, regardless of what the dream is. Whether or not that leap lands you in the *Daily Mail* doesn't matter. At least you won't be left stewing in the comments, wondering what could have been.

The first time I went viral for the wrong reasons was in 2018. I was in Lake Tahoe on a photoshoot for a beer company. When we wrapped for the day, the crew went back to our shared Airbnb, where I crashed down onto one of the beds and opened my Instagram.

Immediately, I was met with dozens and dozens of comments and messages saying that people wanted to "come and shoot my dogs," that I should "do the world a favor and go kill myself."

Sweat wept from every single pore simultaneously. It felt like there was cotton in my ears. I even began muttering out loud, *"Wait wait wait..."*

I racked my brain trying to think if I had set a national forest on fire somewhere and forgotten about it. I couldn't imagine what else would elicit that kind of response.

Very quickly I realized I was being tagged beneath a single post from an Instagram account called @PublicLandsHateYou.

I knew this account. It was started largely in response to a super bloom of wildflowers in California. Influencers (now an official and deeply stigmatized term) had flocked from all over to take whimsical photos of themselves lying in the flowers, pretending to read books, and twirling around in beautiful designer dresses. Problem was, they were doing most of this *off* the trail, resulting in entire patches of flowers being trampled flat.

The internet—sadly—foamed at the mouth. @PublicLandsHateYou was really the first *big* account built on the basis of...bullying. (At least in the outdoor industry realm of social media.) The comment section was scathing and cruel. And I'm ashamed to say that I followed that account before I was a feature on it. I'm still on the fence about whether or not I believe in karma, but I'll never rule it out entirely.

The photo they had shared was of Dagwood and me standing beneath a small arch on the back side of Arches National Park. The rule was that dogs were not to leave the pavement and they had to be on a leash. I had let Dagwood walk up the sandy hill from the road to the base of the arch *purely* for Neil to take that photo. He was not on a leash. So I really *was* in the wrong.

Though if someone had just pointed it out instead of threatening to kill my dogs, I would likely have been much more receptive. (All these years later, the internet still can't seem to grasp the concept that no one is going to listen to you when you start off a sentence with "Go kill yourself.")

Despite immediately knowing that I was the one at fault, I got wildly defensive because that's a pretty realistic human response when it feels like it's twenty-five thousand to one.

Regardless, I still couldn't believe that *that* photo was *that* big of a deal. I hadn't tagged the location or said a single thing about Arches National Park. I wasn't encouraging anyone to go to where I was or do what I was doing. Frankly, it was such a remote part of the park, I was surprised anyone even recognized it. (The defensive twentysomething in me is still alive and well, can't you tell?!)

Nevertheless, I had done something wrong, and the internet was going to make sure I knew all about it, every moment of every day. I deleted the photo from my own page, but that didn't matter, since it had already been plastered on multiple other accounts that were dedicated exclusively to siccing the bored, inexplicably seething masses on public figures.

The angry messages and death threats got so bad that I deactivated my entire account. You couldn't even search for my Instagram. Disappear was the only thing I could think to do, and I'd always been damn good at it, even back then.

I couldn't stay gone for as long as I would have liked. By then, I had made this my only source of income, and it was most certainly a freelance, hustling, paycheck-to-paycheck kind of deal. Instagram does not offer severance packages. After a little over a month, I reactivated my account.

When I did, I decided to publicly own my mistake so I could show people what happened in response to it. I posted screenshots of every direct message I received and every vile comment that the owner of the account had liked or encouraged. (Of course, the owner hid his identity like all the other big, bad wolves on the internet.) But if they wanted to talk about what *I* did, then I was going to make sure everyone knew what they did too.

In response, @PublicLandsHateYou actually faced pretty serious backlash. The official Leave No Trace organization, which had originally made mention of this account in its earliest days, came out and publicly denounced any and all support for it, saying they would not be associated with anyone encouraging violence or bullying. They even announced that they had returned a donation the page's owner had made to them.

Leave No Trace didn't name me in the post, but most folks in the comment section were confident they knew what had caused this quick about-face.

> This is because of what happened to that Brianna Madia chick.

That girl with the dogs was getting death threats from the @PublicLandsHateYou post!

And, of course, there were the handful of folks on there who still believed I should do the world a service and kill myself for this indiscretion.

Regardless, I felt like I had taken a stand, maybe even established myself as someone not to fuck with, for lack of a more eloquent phrase. Even the @PublicLandsHateYou account had to do damage control, posting a new set of "rules" for how to *properly* hate strangers.

When I reactivated my account, I realized that post and the ensuing fallout had gotten me even *more* followers, though I feared the majority of these new ones were simply following along to find more things to be upset about. And, boy, did they ever.

Some folks scrolled back months and months, commenting on every photo of Bucket and Dagwood in any slot canyon or random shotgun-shell-ridden field where free-range cattle had stomped the cryptobiotic soil into dust, declaring, You are violating park laws! Your dogs are ruining the environment!!!!

This is about the time that I came to grips with how confidently people on the internet speak about things they know next to nothing about. Utah has 2.4 million acres of public land run by the Bureau of Land Management. The dirt roads, the canyons, the overlooks, the muddy rivers . . . it's hard to fathom that it ever comes to an end . . . that it doesn't just stretch out forever in every direction. The entire

American Southwest is 60 percent public land. Wild places outnumber the civilized.

As time goes on, people seem less and less inclined to believe that kind of freedom still exists. They assume you must be breaking the rules in order to run naked through the desert with your dogs for weeks, months, years on end...

After the @PublicLandsHateYou debacle, I should have known I wasn't cut out for life in the public eye. The opinions of strangers pierced my skin as if it were made of wet paper. But was I really going to give up and walk away from all of this just because of a handful of assholes who lurked in the shadowy bowels of the internet?

By the end of 2017, I had quit my full-time job to try and make a go at being an author. I had even signed on with a literary agent, who was guiding me through the process of how to start my first memoir.

Bucket and Dagwood spent their days lazing about in the sand, chasing jackrabbits, digging holes, and wading through silty, chocolate-milk-colored rivers while I sat on the riverbank, typing furiously. The ever-present sand beneath the keyboard made it sound more like a typewriter.

With a few sponsorships from companies on Instagram, I had successfully figured out how to live in my van and watch my dogs run free every day. The cattle and the coyotes were our only neighbors. I didn't have utility bills, or appointments, or meetings. The "real world" was a distant memory.

The "real world" only came to me in the sound of screeching

brakes and bloodcurdling screams after Dagwood rolled beneath one of Bertha's thirty-five-inch tires on October 13, 2018. Neil was driving when he hit him. I was in the passenger seat.

But regardless of whose hands were on the wheel, it was still myself that I blamed. I had developed an addiction to watching Bucket and Dagwood soaring through those landscapes as if they had always been a part of them. I had to let them run whenever they wanted to, whenever they shifted, whenever they whined.

That's why we started letting them out to run alongside the van while we slowly rumbled along dirt back roads. Dagwood was only out there running alongside the van that day because I couldn't stand a single second that that dog wasn't free.

After thirty-one days at a veterinary hospital, six surgeries, two blood transfusions, one MRSA infection, and laser therapy to help heal the skin that had been torn open, he was finally discharged. He left that day with the official title of Single Most Expensive Patient in the Clinic's Thirty-Five-Year History.

His nearly *six-figure* medical bills were paid for by over seven thousand individual donations to a GoFundMe page that my mother and a friend had made. They did not mention that Neil was driving, because Neil and I could barely mention it to each other, let alone the public at large.

Dagwood was more than halfway through death's door by the time we arrived at that hospital. There was no time to craft some sort of PR statement. There was no time for anything. I was on my knees on the cold lobby floor, the screen of my phone soaked with tears, as I *pleaded* with my bank to increase my credit limit. I remember the way the receptionists looked at me from behind the desk, heartbroken, helpless.

I have very little memory of even finding out that the GoFundMe existed in the first place. It all happened so fast. But it would go on to haunt my life. I suspect it will for the rest of it.

Because when I came out with the truth that it was *our* van that had hit him, it ignited a firestorm of internet hate that made anything I'd experienced via some public-shaming nature account seem like a breeze.

People called me a liar and a fraud and a scammer and an animal abuser. They said there was "no way his medical bills cost that much." (Before I wrote a check for twenty-three thousand dollars on the fifth day of his hospitalization, I would have said the same thing.) Some folks even claimed that we "hit him on purpose to make money."

People said I should have told the truth right away, and in retrospect I agree with them. But I had mere *seconds* to make decisions. He had already had multiple seizures from blood loss. Every breath was certain to be his last. I was terrified that people wouldn't help Dagwood if they knew we were at fault. And it just wasn't fair to let him pay for *our* mistake with *his* life.

So I chose him over the truth.

By the time we left that hospital, my Instagram was more popular than ever. Thousands upon thousands of people had heard the story of this dog who was beating all the odds in real time.

The comments beneath the updates I'd post about Dagwood's recovery were overwhelmingly positive (he was a literal medical miracle, after all), but tucked in between those thousands of well wishes were a handful of strangers who believed there would *never* be enough penance I could pay for what had happened.

I became known across the internet as "the girl who hit her dog," while Neil shrank back and hid like he always had. Not only had he left me to fend for myself, but to fend for him too, especially when he started to go into a complete tailspin.

All the while, I kept posting about our life, because it felt as though people had paid tickets to see it in the form of the donations they'd made to Dagwood. I felt like I *owed* myself to others, no matter the cost to myself or my marriage. The show had to go on.

I was now dependent on my public platform for my income. I couldn't imagine going back to a gray, drab office every morning, staring longingly out the window like a caged bird . . . leaving Bucket and Dagwood in some apartment all day long, wondering what happened to their life.

Not to mention, if I just up and left Instagram, it would only fuel the rumors that we had stolen the GoFundMe money to go on a Carnival Cruise or whatever other insane shit the internet would come up with day after day. I felt completely backed into a corner.

But above anything else, I didn't want to feel forced to disappear, because I believed in the story I was telling, and I *loved* telling it. I loved when people stopped me on the sidewalk or sent me lengthy messages about how my perspective on life had changed theirs entirely. That was such an honor.

So I dug my heels in and kept doing what I had always done. I kept posting photos of my dogs on Instagram and writing stories about getting Dagwood back to the desert, despite the comment section filling with more and more vicious remarks from more and more anonymous accounts.

By the time I left Neil and moved down to Moab eight years after first downloading Instagram, there was an entire "community" on the website Reddit dedicated exclusively to hating me. They called it MadiaSnark.

I'm sure most folks assumed—and likely still do—that I set out to become *famous* from the very beginning, that this was the plan all along. But all I ever wanted was to be a writer out in the desert with my dogs.

You see, it used to be that if you wanted fame and recognition, you'd move to Hollywood, or go to auditions, or practice roles, or perfect whatever your "talent" was before presenting it to *anyone*. But ending up "famous" on the internet (for both good and bad reasons) can happen in a matter of seconds. It can happen overnight while your phone is plugged in beside your bed.

And when you wake up, it doesn't matter if you wanted it or not. Societally, it's open season. You're fair game. Let the lions into the coliseum. The crowd goes wild.

What did you expect?

chapter three

Never Leave the Dogs Behind

In my earliest days on Instagram, "Never leave the dogs behind" was what I had written as my bio at the top of the page. It was my mantra for bringing Bucket and Dagwood on all of our weekend adventures, no matter how *adventurous* they were. From multiday backpacking trips through the Idaho mountains, to rafting down the Colorado River, to rappelling with us through slot canyons in their specialized technical harnesses . . .

The biggest drop we ever did with them was a whopping 210 feet. The funniest drop we ever did with them was when there was a small crowd of tourists milling about beneath the final sixty-foot descent. A man with a thick New Jersey accent yelled up, "Is that a fuckin' dawg?!"

They were always with me, even if it complicated logistics in a dozen different ways. (Trust me it did.) But it didn't matter. They were *always* with me.

Because everything I've done, I've done for my dogs. Perhaps that sounds like hyperbole, but their happiness has been at the center of every major (and most minor) decision I've made in my adult life. They have always been the compass by which I steer. I mapped the course all the way back one afternoon as I watched them all sleeping in the shade of the junipers.

Most people graduate college with their sights set on a career, but I hadn't thought much about that. I've always been a bit of a "come what may" kind of person. All I could think about was getting my own dog, but my mother had made me promise to wait until I graduated. So just a few days after I was handed my diploma, I was handed a lanky, brindle, seven-month-old mutt from the local animal shelter in Connecticut.

Pet-friendly apartments that a twenty-one-year-old with no career plan could afford were few and far between, so Bucket grew up on a sailboat that Neil's parents owned. Sounds posh, I'm sure, but this was our first encounter with a life void of amenities like running water or temperature control. But I'd have rather lived on that musty old sailboat with Bucket than anywhere in the world without her. She was the center of my universe.

In the fall of 2012, Neil, Bucket, and I shuttered the sailboat and moved west to Utah, sight unseen. It was beautiful and rugged and wild and unlike anything I'd ever been around. That's exactly how I would describe Dagwood when I just happened to walk by him at a Petco adoption event. I was only there to get dog food for Bucket . . . but there he was: a golden-furred, pointy-eared, fifty-some-odd-pound dog frantically digging at the corner of a black kennel, panting, panicked, and trapped—a feeling I've known all too well in my life. A feeling I could see when he finally locked eyes with me through the bars of the cage.

His adoption paperwork said "shepherd mix," but I've never cared a lick about breeds, so I didn't think much of it. He had torn up just about *everything* in our four-hundred-square-foot apartment by the time I learned he was a Carolina dog: a primitive breed discovered living as a free-roaming population by I. Lehr Brisbin Jr. as recently as the 1970s. They are often called American dingoes or Dixie dingoes, due to their physical similarities to the wild dingoes of Australia.

Carolina dogs are just about as *dog* as a dog can get. They're highly active, need constant exercise and stimulation, and have an exquisitely sharp prey drive. Just about *the* worst dog to keep in a second-story studio apartment. It made sense to me now why putting Dagwood on a leash felt . . . wrong. Bucket was on a leash plenty often back when we lived in Connecticut, but Dagwood looked visibly heavier, head sloped downward, eyes low and almond-gold, but missing the light.

It felt like watching a lion being made to do laps around a ring beneath a circus tent. The leashes aren't *hurting* the lions . . . it's just that lions don't belong there in the first place.

So, every weekend, I started making the drive from Salt Lake City down to the desert, long before we had even bought Bertha. The Wasatch Mountain range was mere minutes from our apartment . . . and from a few thousand other peoples' apartments. The trails were crowded and Dagwood had a bit of a humping problem. *Has*, I should say, because at the time of this writing, he is a few months shy of fourteen and still gives it his all.

The dogs and I would cruise past the national parks in favor of those desolate stretches of BLM land that framed them. Not by choice at first, but out of necessity. I had to let Dagwood "run it out" before we tried to integrate into any sort of orderly place with crowds or lines or rules.

Then after a while . . . those places just didn't seem appealing anymore. The postcard-worthy views weren't worth the cost of my dogs' freedom, because their freedom had become my purpose.

They dictated each turn, each decision, each not-very-well-thought-out financial endeavor. Hell, they were asleep at my feet when I stood up abruptly from my desk to quit my office job to go live in a van in the desert. I couldn't wait to run back in and tell them that we were *free*.

For almost a decade, it was the four of us: Bucket, Dagwood, Neil, and me. But in March of 2020, a friend sent me a photo of a dog that had been found dodging tractor trailers on a lone stretch of freeway near the Utah-Colorado border. She was black-and-white speckled with a look in her eyes that could only be described as a yearning.

The Good Samaritans who found her agreed to meet at a rest stop halfway between our locations. Neil and I drove over the mountain pass and down into a small high-desert town where a couple in a Chevron parking lot held a quivering, elf-eared, forty-pound dog that I would come to call Birdie.

The intention was not for it to become "the five of us," the intention was to foster her as a distraction from both my imploding marriage and the global pandemic that brought everything to a screeching halt—including the support groups that I'd been attending and the outpatient program that had been keeping Neil sober.

The result was that we walked on eggshells around each other, as if in limbo, waiting for the next therapist or counselor or book or website to tell us what to say, what to talk about, what to do next. What step comes after twelve?

On the drive back to Salt Lake City that day, we sat in the same uncomfortable silence that we had on the way down. Only now, Birdie was on my lap, melting into the shape of me, resting the full weight of her head on my shoulder, as if she couldn't get close enough. Neil stared out over the steering wheel, quiet and dull-eyed. The only sound I could hear was Birdie's heart thumping in her chest right there next to mine.

Less than two weeks later, when I packed the van up and drove away, Birdie was the one thing on board that had *only* ever been mine. She loved me *so* much that in brief moments, I'd forget how much other people didn't. Perhaps even more than me, she was head over heels for Bucket and Dagwood, assimilating into the role of annoying little sister just perfectly.

By the end of 2020, the new-and-improved "four of us" were up on the mesa on the patch of desert we now called home. It would be a *huge* undertaking to build on, especially for someone like me, who knew not *one* thing about construction or loans or drilling wells. But that didn't matter. I did it for them. They deserved their own piece of wild.

My youngest, Banjo, came the following year as one of the foster puppies toddling behind me as we roved the property day after day. He was just seven weeks old at the time and could fit in my two cupped hands.

Despite being one in a litter of eight, there was just something about the way he locked eyes with me. Something pulled me to him the same way I've been pulled toward all of my dogs. By then, I'd learned not to question that feeling. By then, it was more of a *knowing* than a feeling.

I never intended to end up with more than two dogs, let alone four. I was only planning to foster Birdie and Banjo (and all his siblings) until I found them good homes. Bucket and Dagwood were my whole world, and I was afraid to divert any attention away from them. But the playfulness of Birdie and Banjo brought out a playfulness in Bucket and Dagwood (who were nine and ten at the time). I figured if they helped to raise Birdie and Banjo, they would always be a part of them in some way. Then Birdie and Banjo would help raise the next, and so on and so forth. If the chain was never broken, I could have Bucket and Dagwood forever.

. . .

My dogs have always been my everything, but for a long time, they were my only thing. The only thing I had that was worth sticking around for.

"Never leave the dogs behind" devolved from a cute adventure mantra into something much darker in the wake of my divorce. All four of them would pile into bed with me as I cried, while the very dog those folks online all claimed to be so concerned about diligently licked the tears they were causing.

In every moment that I intended to be my last, I would look down at them and see four reasons that I *had* to live. Not that I should. That I *had* to. I loved them more than I loved myself.

What I did to keep Dagwood alive all those years earlier should have been a testament to that, but I became "the girl who hit her dog," not "the girl who *saved* her dog." The miraculous work done by his veterinarians, the support of so many kind strangers, and my undying love for him was overshadowed by semantics. By the difference between an omission and a lie.

And little do those folks know that if it came down to it, I would have done far worse. I would have lied, cheated, stolen, said anything, done anything to save that dog from what was nothing more than a tragic accident. But perhaps even more tragic is this: Anyone who claims they wouldn't have done the same hasn't been lucky enough to love a dog as much as I do.

chapter four

My Beach

Moab in July is not for the weak. Living in a trailer without running water or air-conditioning meant the dogs and I survived off of a small, solar-powered fan during the night, and sitting neck-deep in the muddy Colorado during the day.

I had found a beach on the opposite side of the river, only accessible by water. It wasn't even visible until the snowmelt ran out and the water level dropped. With each passing summer day, the river narrowed, slipping lower and lower to reveal a strip of sand tucked beneath a towering red wall, framed with seep willow, swaying grasses, and one single cottonwood tree whose roots must have had to hold on for dear life for it to get to that size. Flash floods, erosion, and extreme heat makes *anything's* ability to thrive in the desert pretty noteworthy.

In order to get to said beach, I'd park a little ways upriver from it and inflate my paddleboard on the side of the road. The heat coming off the pavement was so intense that I often wondered if it might compromise the rubber.

I forced the dogs to wait in the car with the AC blasting as sweat ran down my face and arms, manually pumping up my half-melting board. Once inflated, I'd strap a soft-sided cooler to the front and tow a waterproof backpack from the rear, attached with a dog leash. Next, and most importantly, came the dogs. They knew the drill well and waited as I strapped their lifejackets on one by one by one by one before they got the okay to jump out and head for the board.

Banjo had been riding on a paddleboard since he was eight weeks old, so he often jumped onto it with such enthusiasm that he'd unintentionally push himself off from the shore as if he was going to set sail on his own. I'd wade out through the lukewarm, muddy water to catch him before the current did.

Bucket always got her place in the front of the paddleboard, followed by Birdie, me, Banjo, then Dagwood bringing up the rear. Once we were all loaded up, the top of the board was *just* about level with the water itself. I'd sit with my legs dangling over on either side, as if riding it like a horse. I'm sure it looked like an absolute clown car, but I preferred to think of it as more of a Huck Finn–esque adventure. Slap some stuff together and hope it floats.

The importance of starting upriver from the beach cannot be understated. If I had tried to paddle over from directly across, the current would take us, and we'd miss it. Then we'd just be stuck floating our way toward the next town, and who knows where the hell that would be.

In the summer of 2021, the water level was so low that I would tie a dog leash around one of the paddleboard straps and drag us across the river, my feet sinking into the mud with each step. The water was so cloudy that you couldn't see your own hand beneath two inches of it.

On the first foot crossing to the beach that summer, I'd walked straight into a sandbar that shot up abruptly at the centermost point of the river, causing the paddleboard to smash into my back. The dogs all lurched forward. Banjo rolled off unintentionally, but Bucket stood up and leapt in of her own accord, seemingly annoyed at my incompetence. Lord knows she could swim faster than I could walk through chest-deep water.

By the time we'd land on shore, one could have mistaken us for having been lost at sea for weeks. Bags bobbing off the sides of the board, empty water bottles rolling off the rubber, bodies soaking wet and covered in mud from the knees down. Exhausted, I'd drag the board up and collapse onto the ground, blinking in the bluebird sky above.

The dogs would shake the water from their fur and take off in either direction down the beach, which was maybe only a hundred feet long and tucked into a curve of sandstone where the river rounded a corner.

Since the water dropped by the day, the first bit of shoreline was almost always slicked with a layer of mud, but the dogs and I didn't mind at all. I loved the way it felt between my toes. It was almost always dotted with trails of huge webbed footprints; a telltale sign that the great blue herons were near.

Sometimes there would even be winding drag marks from the

tail of a beaver making his way up toward that singular cottonwood tree. I liked to think that our near daily presence on the beach might keep him at bay . . . keep my tree from succumbing to that fate.

I say "my tree" because the only name I'd ever come up with for this little stretch of sand was My Beach. Mostly because it was the easiest thing to say when my mother would call and ask what I was up to that day.

"Me and the dogs are going out to My Beach."

"Again?" she'd ask.

"Again."

I opened my Instagram one afternoon as I sat at the mouth of the road that led to the beach. There was one dirt pull-off that I'd always use to check any happenings on my phone before disappearing out of service for the remainder of the day. There were usually *plenty* of happenings.

Every time I opened the app, there was another fake username made to mock me or a message about how I was the world's worst dog owner or the biggest bitch on the planet or whatever new thing they would come up with day after day after day.

Regardless, that morning I scrolled through my messages, dodging the vulgar ones from anonymous accounts, until I landed on a name I recognized. He'd never sent me a message before, but we did follow each other. *William . . . William . . .* I jogged my mind trying to remember where we'd met, but only for a moment as the second line of his message answered that.

It was a film premiere in 2018. The outdoor gear company Patagonia had sponsored a handful of us to run a relay race across Bears Ears National Monument in southern Utah. At the time, Trump was trying (successfully, it turned out) to remove its national monument status, essentially opening it up for drilling and livestock.

The race was organized by a friend, Len, a member of the Navajo Nation who had gone on to become a professor of indigenous studies at a college in Arizona. His mother met us where the baked red road wove up right between the two giant rock formations that gave the place its name, a place they considered sacred.

She and Len ran that leg together.

William hadn't run in the race, but was there to watch the film about it. We had plenty of mutual friends, so I'm assuming that's why we started following each other on Instagram, and were apparently still following each other all these years later.

He was asking for some pointers on locations for a photoshoot he had coming up the following week.

"Ohhh, that's right, this is the photographer guy," I murmured aloud to Birdie as she sat beside me in the front seat, itching to get on our way.

I scrolled through his profile briefly before deciding he was too good-looking not to answer. He had acquired a decent following on Instagram as well, given the gorgeous photos he posted from his adventures all over the world.

I listed off a few spots that would fit the scenery he said he was aiming for. He thanked me, and mentioned that he would be in town the day before the shoot to scout the locations. He said he would love to meet up if I was around.

I wrote back: Yea I'd love to, let me know when you get in!

Then I sent him my phone number, knowing full well that scrolling through my land-mine-filled Instagram messages was the *last* place I wanted to communicate with anyone.

I figured he wouldn't reach out. I figured he was just being polite. Like running into some old acquaintance and saying "We should get together sometime!" but you know full well it's just a formality.

The following Thursday, I awoke with a vicious hangover inside a trailer whose internal temperature had surpassed eighty degrees by 9 a.m. But whether I was hungover or not, the daily routine remained the same. Unless it was a cloudy day (rare) or a flash flood (even more rare), every day was spent at My Beach.

Bertha had been broken down for months beside a juniper tree, seeping transmission fluid into a catch pan, so everything had to fit in my Jeep Wrangler, which is a very capable vehicle, but quite small when you've upgraded to four dogs. Banjo loved to sit on top of the rolled-up, deflated paddleboard for a better view out the window. He was still only a few months old at the time.

My clown car full of dogs and gear rolled down the mesa, out onto the pavement, and twenty or so miles north into town. I swung by the Dollar Store to throw my trash into their dumpster before pulling up to my favorite coffee drive-thru. While waiting, my phone started vibrating incessantly, a sign that I had officially left the blissfully service-free world of my property and reentered the chaotic one.

An unknown number had sent me a text.

Hey Bri, it's William. Just got to town, where should we meet up?

"*Fffffffuck...*" I whispered aloud. I guess he was serious...

My fingers hovered over the keyboard as my headache thumped like a heartbeat in both temples. I was tempted to say I couldn't, but I was even more tempted to not say anything at all. When the place you *live* has no cell service or Wi-Fi, "not getting someone's message" is an extremely valid excuse after all.

I grabbed a few Advil from the bottle in my glove box and swallowed them down with a sip of coffee, took a deep breath, and immediately gave him an out.

I'm actually heading out toward the river with my dogs.
I paddle us across to this beach every day. It's kind of a shitshow getting over there...

He responded with something about how hot it was out and how nice going to a beach would be. I wrote back something that surprised even me in the moment.

If you don't have a kayak or a paddleboard, I can probably figure out a way to get us all across.

He agreed without hesitation and said he would wait for me at a different coffee shop in town.

As someone who hadn't had an in-depth conversation with a human person in ages, let alone spent an entire afternoon with one, I was immediately overcome with anxiety. I pulled into the nearest gas station and ran inside to the bathroom while the dogs waited in the AC of the running car like they did during all of my errands.

Leaning my hands on the cold porcelain sink, I stared at the absolute mess of a reflection looking back at me. My eyes were bloodshot, hair matted, skin tanned to a leathery brown. I wore nothing but shorts and a bathing suit top and a pair of Chacos permanently caked in river mud. I should point out that this is not at all unusual as Moab is rife with van-dwelling dirtbags and climbers who consider baby wipes to be sufficient as a shower. Though I'm not one to talk, considering that I was not above spraying myself off at the car wash, which is also where I did my dishes in an old Home Depot bucket.

Despite the fact that the woman I saw in the mirror looked quite a mess, I still saw *myself*. Even through the dust and dirty clothes and damn-near-dreadlocked hair. For much of the last year, looking in the mirror was practically an out-of-body experience. I hadn't recognized my face in a very long time.

I splashed cold water on my cheeks and attempted to fluff my hair at the scalp with my fingertips before mumbling, "Ugh, whatever, it's not like you're gonna marry this guy..."

Back in the car, I turned to face the dogs. "Don't... embarrass me," I said through gritted teeth.

When we pulled into the coffee shop parking lot, the dogs erupted in barking from behind my dark-tinted windows as William climbed out of his car and started walking our way.

I had forgotten (or maybe never even noticed before) how tall he was. When I hugged him hello, I couldn't help but *ask* how tall he was.

"Six five on a good day." He smiled.

He had long blond hair that hung down past his shoulder blades and striking blue eyes and a short, scruffy beard. His legs were strong, tanned, and covered in tattoos. He looked, for lack of a better description, like a Viking.

I felt... nervous.

"So, what's the game plan?" he asked, peering over my shoulder at the car full of barking dogs.

I took a deep breath and chuckled. "Well, there's no way *you* of all people are fitting in there with us, so you'll have to drive separately... if you still want to come."

I found myself giving him a last-minute out, despite feeling a flush in my cheeks when we'd lock eyes. I'd have been perfectly happy out there alone like I always was. But he pulled the keys from his pocket.

"I'll follow you!" he shouted as he climbed back into his rental car.

I stared over the steering wheel, not playing any music, which was unusual. But this entire situation felt unusual. Out of character for whoever I had become those days, which was—as so aptly described in *Grey Gardens*—a bit of a "society dropout."

I didn't do small talk and meetups and lunches with friends. In that town, I *had* no friends. I'd only built a few bridges when I arrived in Moab in the midst of the Covid pandemic, and I'd successfully reduced all of them to ashes by the year's end. As soon as someone tried to get close, I'd sabotage it or, more commonly, decide one day to simply never respond again, which I believe the young folks call "ghosting."

Because, like most people in the immediate wake of a bitter divorce, I swore that I'd never love again. And having been made a target online meant that friendships were out of the question too. I didn't trust *anyone* to keep the things I said or did a secret. There was an entire online forum for people to share "information" about me.

Faraway friends were the only ones I had left. Though I still battled the paranoia that even people I'd known and loved since grade school might be posting about me from some fake account.

There was absolutely no evidence to believe that they would do something like that, but when there's an entire "community" dedicated to hating you, you start to believe there *must* be something really worth hating. I must *deserve* this.

Given that my ability to trust anyone or anything had all but vanished, it was wildly out of character for me to be leading what might as well have been a perfect stranger to one of the safest, most solitary places I had. Though I did take into account that my idea of the perfect place is quite a bit different than most. I had come to set the same expectations as my dogs. A half-sand, half-mud beach all to ourselves was heaven.

As William stood over me in the blazing hot sun, I was confident this wasn't his idea of heaven. He asked if there was anything he could do to help, to which I said no, of course. By then, I'd become extremely protective of my chaos. I didn't care if I was doing things the "right" way or the most "efficient" way. So long as it was *my* way, which was, as you might have guessed ... chaotic.

He stood there silently, smiling, and eventually sidestepping so that the shade of his towering figure would at least protect me from *some* sun.

I pulled and pressed the manual pump up and down, up and down, sweat rolling off my face and down my spine. I could have bought an electric pump at any number of stores in Moab, but the manual labor had become something I was weirdly attached to. When I paused to catch my breath and wipe my forehead, he looked on silently.

Now, some folks might hear that and think of it as just another headstone in the graveyard of chivalry, but I was ... intrigued. I did not want to be "taken care of," or treated as if I couldn't do everything myself, because I *had* to do everything myself. Including being the captain of this jerry-built vessel that would need to carry two large humans (I'm quite tall myself, I should mention) as well as four dogs and a cooler and some drybags for things like phones and speakers and such.

I explained the order of operations to William, gesturing like Vanna White toward each area of the paddleboard that was about to be completely overtaken by wet dogs. On days this hot, they always ran right into the water before leaping aboard for the crossing, soaking everything in a matter of seconds as if with a hose.

He put his hands on his hips and laughed.

"Where do you want me?"

The easiest thing to do was to have him take his seat on the board first, which would be exactly how I rode it: butt on the paddleboard, legs in the water on either side. When I opened the Jeep door, the dogs sent a Tasmanian devil's amount of dust up into the air before taking four flying leaps directly onto the board. *At least they stayed dry,* I thought to myself, watching William's eyes dart from dog to dog.

They remained dry for about twenty seconds before the splash of what was likely a beaver tail sent them careening off toward the murky shoreline, nearly knocking William off the board entirely. When they got back on, they were now wet *and* muddy. This, of course, was a completely unremarkable part of my day. Everything I owned was covered in mud and dog hair, including the bed I slept in every night. But I found myself feeling a tiny bit self-conscious at William's reaction, which could best be described as a sort of stunned silence.

Not wanting to make the board any more overwhelming, I decided I would just swim us across. The water flow was low enough to no longer shift the sandbars, meaning I'd memorized where they were; my feet sliding over the bottom as if reading braille with my toes.

I explained that I'd really only need to "swim" us for the first forty feet (a.k.a. swim out in front of the board, dragging it behind me with a dog leash tethered to the front handle).

The extra 210 pounds from this man was . . . palpable. I swam forward, then flipped over on my back to face the board, my feet kicking beneath it now. It was quite the image. A man being dragged across the river by some swamp woman with four muddy dogs in multicolored lifejackets. Banjo sat his little wet self directly on William's lap, gazing up at him every now and again.

When my feet reached the sandbar, William jumped off the board and we waded together through the chest-deep water. I think he'd had enough of the Driving Miss Daisy routine.

The dogs were off and tearing down the beach within seconds, leaving the two of us alone. In that instant, the difference between the frantic scramble getting here and the sudden hush of arrival was striking. It felt as if someone had abruptly cut the power to a booming soundtrack, leaving the two of us beside each other in a daze.

It was too hot to sit beside the water, so we found a sandy spot where we could lie half in and half out.

"I told you there's a reason we sit 'neck-deep' in here all day." I laughed.

William reclined, propped himself up on his tanned arms, and scanned the river side to side. Then he leaned back to look up at the wall behind us so it was all topsy-turvy, the blue sky and red stone reversed. He exuded an extraordinary sense of calm that I found both magnetic and unnerving. But the silence was unbearable for me, despite how totally content he seemed with it.

It felt like a violation, given that silence was where I had been most comfortable for a long time. I had never once sat on that beach before and thought, *What do I say?* Besides the dogs and the blue herons (who are notoriously poor conversationalists), there was no one to say anything to.

"Do you mind if I put on some music?" I blurted out, a little too frantically. "Do you like country music?"

He looked over at me with a smile. "I grew up on a farm. Country is pretty much all I listen to."

I put on Nitty Gritty Dirt Band's "Fishin' in the Dark" and took advantage of the conversation prompt he'd just offered. Asking someone where they're from is a pretty normal way to start, so you'd have thought it would be covered by now, but the morning hit us pretty hard. I don't think we exchanged a single pertinent detail about ourselves until we got to the other side of that river. Two relative strangers, stuck on an island that I had swum us to.

But his voice was deep and measured, his words well chosen.

It was a chicken farm in a small town in central Illinois. A *real* farm with a big red barn and a towering silo, framed by cornfields and a smattering of cows. He and his younger sister grew up doing proper farm chores, like collecting eggs and cleaning coops.

"When I was a kid, we had Drive Your Tractor to School Day," he said, smiling out at the water as if he could still see it now.

"How small is this town?!" I laughed, incredulously.

"Couple hundred people when I was growing up, but I haven't lived there since before college. Though I doubt it's experienced any sort of major population boom since then."

He paused. "You're from the East Coast, right?"

It was only then that I remembered that we *did* follow each other on Instagram. I wasn't a complete mystery to him, which should not have been a complete mystery to me, given that I had over a quarter of a million followers online at that point. Commonly suggested Google searches for my name included:

Brianna Madia reddit
Brianna Madia divorce
Brianna Madia Dagwood accident
Brianna Madia GoFundMe
Brianna Madia's husband dead?
What happened to Brianna Madia

And while I'm absolutely *certain* William had never googled me, even a brief scroll through my Instagram those days was like peering into the window of a house that was burning down. I had only recently decided that I didn't want to burn down with it, but there was still ash on my skin and the smell of smoke in my hair as I sat beside him on the beach that day.

He indicated that he *did* know about Dagwood's accident. Therefore, I knew he knew about the *very* public fallout.

I was torn between feeling embarrassed and feeling . . . relieved. Having to tell that *entire* complicated, traumatic story over and over and over again was exhausting. A few times I had reverted to the response I used to get people off my back, to keep burying the burden that came along with the truth.

"He got hit by *a* car," I'd say hurriedly. "They had to amputate his tail, but he's totally fine now, it was a long time ago."

I had to reassure myself that that was okay. That I didn't owe the entire story to every stranger passing by on a trail, that I didn't have to beg them for forgiveness.

William knew about it. Not in great detail, of course, but he knew the most important parts. Dagwood got hit. And Dagwood lived.

Regardless, I still found myself pining for a time when I could introduce myself the way I used to be able to before Dagwood's accident. Before Instagram entirely. I wished I had control over what information to share and when to share it and who was even worthy of having an opinion about it.

Because I suddenly found myself *caring* what William's opinion might be.

The sun cast different shadows on our faces for every hour that it shifted across the sky. We talked about traveling and rock climbing and backpacking and sailboats. I had lived on one. He had just spent twenty-eight days sailing a thirty-one-footer clear across the Pacific Ocean from Washington to Hawaii. (Which explained the perfect tan.) We talked about up and leaving our respective hometowns, which is a brave feat for any young twentysomething, regardless of population size.

This corn-fed, six-foot-five chicken farmer from rural Illinois had one of those extra-large passports with double the pages and damn near all of them stamped. Thirty-six years old and completely untethered. He'd quit his well-paying job as a mechanical engineer in his late twenties to pursue professional photography, and had spent the last eight years living in his own old, frequently broken Volkswagen van named Ruby. She was a 1990 just like Bertha.

It was refreshing to talk to someone who knew what it was to have old vans and what it was to love them (a.k.a. to tolerate them because, somehow, the good still outweighs the bad). I told him I was desperate and determined to get Bertha running again.

"I'm gonna build her out, maybe put a high-top on," I mused, wriggling my toes into the wet sand. "I said I'm gonna do it, so I will." I nodded definitively. At that point, I had a pretty impressive track record on following through, so I had no reason not to wholeheartedly believe my own words.

"I know a whole bunch of guys up in Oregon that would be so stoked to work on that thing!" he said excitedly. It occurred to me then that I'd never heard someone else talk about a broken-down van with such enthusiasm. No one had ever lit up about her the way that I did. Most people looked at her and saw, well . . . a broken-down van. Scrap metal. Too far gone to fix.

"Really?" I said, turning to face him. "I've started setting aside a little bit of money, I just didn't know who to bring it to. I guess the question would be *how* to get her all the way up there, honestly." I laughed. To date, Bertha's longest journey on a tow truck had been from Albuquerque, New Mexico, back to Moab, Utah. Three hundred and seventy-five miles, to be exact. And despite being my longest tow, it wasn't even my most expensive.

One summer afternoon, Bertha's engine quit on me sixty-five miles down a decently bumpy dirt road in the middle of August. The dogs and I sat there, right in the middle of the road, for over twenty hours, chasing the shade around the van as the day droned on and on.

At one point, I saw a haze of dust on the horizon and leapt to my feet, only to find a cow and her calf trotting down the road, headed lord knows where in such a hurry.

By the time I saw the actual tow truck rolling toward us through the rippling heat, I wondered if it was a mirage. But signing for the $2,200 charge to get us back to Moab brought me back to reality quick.

William had more than his fair share of nomadic disaster stories, like the time his transmission blew out completely, stranding him alone in a tiny town in the middle of Canada for almost two weeks. But like me and all the other lovesick drifters, he just couldn't give up the dream.

We sat in the sand, swam, then sat in the sand again, our laughter echoing off the canyon wall. We wandered down to one end of the beach before turning to stroll down to the other, talking all the while. His footprints in the sand dwarfed mine. This was a place reserved for me and the dogs and our particular brand of "doing nothing." But William turned out to be a way better stick thrower than I was, so Birdie and Bucket (my swimmers) weren't bothered by this new addition. Banjo toddled along behind him closely, as if they already knew each other. Dagwood still stuck by me, though.

Dagwood always stuck by me.

Perhaps you're expecting me to launch into a story about how this was all love at first sight, but the feeling that grabbed hold of me that afternoon was closer to fear. In fact, I didn't like the way I felt at all. I preferred the silence of my completely disassociated bubble, where everyone was at a distance, where nothing was real and no one could get to me, regardless of their intention. I'd successfully hidden myself down dirt roads, tucked myself into the cracks of deep canyons, found solace on a beach with the entire Colorado River between me and everything else.

I didn't want to look back and see some man's footprints in the sand beside mine. Four dogs' worth was plenty.

So the following day, when he sent a text asking if I'd like to go swim at one of the boat ramps with him and the rest of the crew after the photoshoot, I never responded. I was *angry* he even asked. I was angry at how my heart fluttered when I saw his name on my phone, like the first signs of life from a moth's wings after a storm.

chapter five

Dirt Road Etiquette

Shortly after buying my property, I decided I was a cowboy. That is to say, my collection of boots and hats grew to overtake each corner of my trailer, *y'all* became an inextricable part of my vocabulary, and '90s country music was just about all I listened to. I even started smoking the occasional cigarette just for effect.

This was all a far cry from my suburban Connecticut upbringing. But I figured living in Utah for over a decade by then had flushed the last of the East Coast from my blood.

Though my mother made sure to remind me that I do, in fact, have a decent amount of "down-home roots." So, waltzin' around dusty back roads in snip-toed boots, singing along to Alan Jackson wasn't quite as unfounded as I may have thought.

My mother's biological father was born, raised, and buried in Macon, Georgia. He was so scarcely in my mother's life that I knew next to nothing about him. The first time I met my biological grandfather, I was twenty-seven years old. When he and my grandmother met back in the 1950s, he was living on his parents' sprawling, overgrown property at the edge of Cherry Lake. They'd spend most of their time fishing and hunting, as evidenced by the legion of hound dogs that would tear through their house, much like that scene from *A Christmas Story*.

My great-grandparents were salt of the earth and rough around the edges, but my grandfather was still raised with a certain idea of what a "good southern woman" should be . . . and that most certainly didn't match my grandmother's balls of steel, hence the marriage didn't last. The fact that my grandmother came out as a lesbian fifty years later also lent some additional insight into why it ended in divorce.

Regardless, one of my favorite old photos is of her in black-and-white, standing in the driveway on that property with a shotgun in one hand, a dead possum by the tail in the other, and a Virginia Slim hanging from her parted lips. In this picture, she's a few months pregnant with my mother.

By 2021, I had this photo pinned up in the trailer on my own property. I was lucky enough to get to tell my grandmother that before she died at the age of eighty-eight.

One afternoon I stopped for gas at a Texaco in southern California. A man held his gaze on me from the adjacent pump as I leaned against my Jeep in a silverbelly Stetson. "Nice hat." He smirked. "Where's your ranch?"

I secretly loved when some smart-ass would hit me with that line, because I got to look them dead in the face and say, "Back up in Utah. Nine acres south of Moab. Where's yours?"

I'm aware that I don't always look the part, or that maybe it looked like I was just *playing* a part, but I'd become a bit of a walking paradox by then. It was as if each facet of who I was somehow contradicted the next.

Connecticut may not have worn off on me, but my mother had, so no matter my living conditions over the years, I've always had a bit of a high-end skincare habit. I'd watch my fifty-five-dollar face wash swirl down the cold metal sink of a highway rest stop before delicately distributing expensive Swedish face oil across my sunburnt cheeks. Why would I waste money on my own running water when just about every public restroom has sinks full of it? And when I needed a head-to-toe shine, it was only five bucks for a shower pass at the Moab Aquatic Center.

It was totally within my financial means to rent an apartment until I could afford to build my house like a normal person, but that would be far less free and far less fun. Not to mention, I never once considered my situation to be dire or unlivable. Uncomfortable at times? Yes, but never unlivable.

When I fostered my first litter of puppies, folks from the Reddit made calls to the shelter, stating that I wasn't fit to foster because I was living without air-conditioning or running water. In turn, the folks at the shelter reminded them that there was *also* no running water under the shed in the baking-hot New Mexico sun where those puppies were found after their mother was hit and killed by a car. They were certain that bottled water would be up to their standard so long as I made sure to ask if they wanted sparkling or still. The insinuation was that my trailer was not fit for a pile of freshly born street dogs.

And yet, the way I was living is the way that billions of people around the world live. Forget *running* water: According to the UN, in 2023 an estimated 46 percent of the planet's population lived without *safe* water or safely managed sanitation. My water may not come out of a faucet, but at least it was drinkable, so thus far, my own dogs and I had been able to survive that *terrible* hardship.

A toilet that's just a simple hole in the floor *or* the ground is not just common, it's mainstream in many parts of the world. I would know: I've watched other tourists look down their noses at bathrooms across the globe from Cambodia to Jordan to Indonesia to Morocco and beyond.

This is the kind of perspective (and gratitude) lost when you allow your life to get easy, when you forget what hard *actually* feels like . . . what things are *actually* worth stressing over. I've seen too many folks mistake their privileges for norms. But I digress . . .

Another thing that rubbed off on me from my mother is the importance of a good wardrobe. Although I've always been enraptured with clothes, with how one can decorate themselves however they see fit. I even applied to a college in New York City to study fashion marketing. I pictured myself expertly navigating cobblestone streets in a pair of heels, or attending hip loft parties and having outfits that "go from day to night" like all the magazines claimed we would need on a pretty regular basis.

Can you fucking imagine?!

Instead, I went to a state school in Rhode Island, where I majored in writing and rhetoric, but when I look at my outstanding student loans all these years later, it feels more like I paid for a forty-thousand-dollar keg stand.

Despite devolving from a New York City–bound fashionista to a woman out in the desert whom the government would officially classify as "without housing," I had still been carting the same four or five boxes of clothes around with me for over a decade.

They'd been shoved into a college closet, a sailboat, a studio apartment, a van, but primarily in an array of storage units across the state of Utah. Most of it was from a brand called Free People. There was a little boutique next to the bookstore I'd hang out in when I would get off the train after high school. The owner came to know me well, as I started saving up as much of my babysitting money as I could to buy Free People from her shop. She even had me babysit her own kids a few times.

The clothes were hand-embroidered and beaded and bohemian and flowy and *messy*. So different from the sea of crisp, collared shirts and Nantucket red shorts, or the Lilly Pulitzer shift dresses that might as well have been strung up on a pole as the Connecticut state flag.

But perhaps, most formatively, it was the first time clothes fit my AA cups perfectly. (To be honest, I'm just estimating that bra size; I've never actually owned one that wasn't made entirely of fabric and sold as small, medium, or large. Underwire support is unnecessary when the weight it's "supporting" is akin to a couple of kiwis.)

It was the first time that almost everything my enviably busty school friends tried on looked far more suited to *my* figure. The clothes hung just right on my "mosquito-bite tits" and my "linebacker shoulders" that the schoolboys snickered about. *My* figure... which was *quite literally* described as "boy-shaped" in the fashion advice columns in *Teen Vogue* and *Seventeen* magazine. (There is a reason that any woman who lived through the early 2000s most likely has some manufactured self-loathing that still haunts her like a pair of low-rise jeans.)

Maybe it sounds a little dramatic to say that a clothing line played a huge role in my high school self-esteem... but it did. Those well-traveled boxes are full of things I've collected over decades, things that make me feel like *me*, regardless of where I happen to be storing them. And thanks to the fact that I'm still waiting to hit puberty at thirty-five, most of them still fit.

Not to mention, you can make any look go from day to night if you're just wandering around your yard.

Though my love for clothes was nothing new, the appointment I made at a med spa for Botox and filler most certainly was. Immediately following my divorce, I was convinced I could turn my whole life around if my top lip was just a *little* bit plumper and I could find the right haircut for my limp, blond curls. The limpness likely came from the fact that I'd been highlighting it religiously since I was in high school, only now I'd go four to five days without washing it. I do have a fancy silk pillowcase, though. It's good for your hair and it's easy to brush the dirt off of before bed.

At the med spa, two women stood over me in what felt like a dentist's chair, pinching and poking, telling me to smile, frown, raise my eyebrows, as if in shock. The diagnosis was that I had your run-of-the-mill, averagely aging forehead, but the crow's feet around my eyes were pretty deep for being only thirty.

They recommended some sort of half-face special for the forehead and the ones around my eyes, which I promptly rejected. *Those* wrinkles I like. I saw those as proof that, despite everything along the way, I had still smiled more than the average thirty-year-old... or maybe I'd just laid in the sun more. But I won't ever stop laying in the sun. I'm a withering plant without it. Sometimes I'm convinced that my life is nothing but a pointless downward spiral until I realize that it's just cloudy out.

So, I sprawl out in the nude on my chaise lounge, baking like a lizard with my freshly paralyzed forehead. I figure if I keep getting Botox, it'll be like two wizards' wands fighting against each other, keeping the progression of my aging forehead suspended somewhere in that same average range it started out in.

Is this a logical, healthy, or effective mindset? Probably not. But this is not a how-to book. Don't look to me as some kind of life coach; I'm better thought of as a drunk aunt.

· · ·

I like to think that financial independence is something that would have rubbed off on me if my mother had ever had it. (Though it's worth mentioning that my mother's idea of a perfect life is not nearly as affordable as mine.) But she was so proud of me for being totally self-sufficient. I didn't have to hide any shopping bags or receipts or credit card statements like we did when I was growing up.

But what mattered more to me than *all* that surface-level fluff was this: Being self-reliant makes it easy to leave.

Dependency is dangerous because relationships are unpredictable. I never intended to spend one moment in a place I no longer cared to be, with a person I no longer cared to be with.

Financial independence was a cornerstone of my belief that the best thing one can do in this life is be ready and able to run.

chapter six

The Taco Truck

Just a few weeks after I met William, running was all I had on my mind.

That day on the beach, we'd talked a lot about Baja, Mexico. He had driven his van down there for the last three consecutive winters.

"I tried to make it down there once," I said, laughing, looking up at the cloudless sky, "but Bertha broke down on the border. You know... old van shit."

Given that Bertha had now been broken down on my property for half a year, it was safe to say I wasn't going to attempt it again. But it occurred to me very suddenly one afternoon that I had a perfectly reliable Jeep, and while I certainly couldn't "live" out of it the way I could have in Bertha, it could at least *get* me there.

"Baja has Airbnbs, right?" I mused aloud to the dogs as I opened the app on my phone.

I left the very next morning because, in case you haven't caught on yet, that's just the way that I am. Better get goin' before you chicken out.

I posted triumphantly on my Instagram that I was going to load the dogs up and drive 1,627 miles from Utah all the way down the Baja peninsula by myself (a.k.a. with the dogs). I had no concrete plans, no existing reservations, and next to no understanding of the Spanish language. But I had already decided I would go. So I went.

The juxtaposition of the landscapes in Baja is hard to wrap your mind around. Caribbean-colored water flush up against baked brown hillsides, dotted with the occasional green saguaro cactus that had survived by rooting itself between the jagged red rocks. Things that look like they're dying of thirst sit just a few dozen paces from a sea so rich in life that Jacques Cousteau called it "the aquarium of the world."

These two extremes coexisted seamlessly, and I immediately loved them both. I loved not knowing if the most desolate-looking road might deposit you into some shimmering blue paradise. I loved the inherent adventure in being aimless. I loved the dead ends and the sun-faded NO TRASPASAR signs rusted to the wire of some old cattle fence. I loved the three-point turns and the U-turns. Hell, I even grew to love the wrong turns.

It wasn't too far off from my life in Utah, only after a long day in the sun, we cooled off in clear blue water as opposed to the murky clay of the Colorado River.

. . .

I had only made it a quarter of the way down the peninsula when William's name popped up on my phone screen again. The first since I'd left him hanging about the post-photoshoot swim.

> Did you stop at the taco truck in Guerrero that I told you about?!

I had just come back into cell service, because it's blissfully fleeting down there like it is on my property. My phone was abuzz with activity. My editor wanted to know if I had any intention of meeting my deadline. My mother wanted to know if I was alive or not.
But the first text I opened was his.
My fingers hovered over the keyboard.

> I'm going to try to make it there tomorrow! I had a hell of a time in Bahia de LA yesterday. Didn't realize the whole town runs only on cash and has no ATM. I had to beg someone to help me fill my gas tank so I could get back to Route 1.

I watched the three little dots as he typed back.

> There will definitely be an ATM in Guerrero! Happens to the best of us . . .

The next day I followed the pin he dropped to the taco truck, where I had what turned out to truly be the most incredible tacos I've ever eaten. Pickled red onions and cabbage sprinkled down onto my bare legs as I scarfed down three of them in the front seat of the Jeep. The dogs were asleep in the back; the air-conditioning gently ruffling their salt-covered fur from the morning swim.

I took out my phone and snapped a photo of the now-empty paper basket that once housed the tacos.

Holy shit. Best tacos I've ever had!

He wrote back immediately.

If you liked those, you'll love the next place in Mulege . . .

He offered up a few beach locations as well, but I didn't visit them on principle. I was down here to do this by *myself*. Any beach I found would be of my own accord. I was, however, grateful for the dining suggestions, as I had almost exclusively been eating gas station food in my car.

By the time I was approaching the southernmost tip of the Baja peninsula several weeks later, William and I had been talking almost every day.

At first, it was just texting back and forth about my trip. He would offer recommendations or make commentary about my Instagram stories or ask if some little bodega was still in some little town. I'd send pictures of the dogs on the beach, or my mezcal margarita with a glittering blue sea full of sailboats for a backdrop. One evening, after *several* of those, I sent him a selfie of me pressed up against Bucket's cheek, smiling in the purply light of sunset.

He wrote back: I'm going to make this your contact photo.

homesick nomad

...

The following morning, I found myself thinking about him. So much so that I narrowly avoided plowing into a few honey-colored cows that had decided to stand in the middle of the road. Banjo lurched forward, pressing his nose to the windshield, barking like Cujo in all of his twenty-pound, five-month-old glory. (It's easy to act tough from the safety of a passing car window.)

They had white noses, those old-fashioned bells around their necks, and the same bored, blank stare that seems to be universal among cows. The cloud of dust from the abrupt stop plumed up around them and in through the car windows, sticking to the sweat on my arms. After three weeks of doing this day after day, I had lost all ability to discern if I was perfectly suntanned or just . . . really dirty.

As the dust cleared, I could see a trail of chalky hoofprints from where the cows had come. I rolled forward slowly, gravel crunching beneath the Jeep's tires, until I reached the mouth of a long, perfectly straight, white sand road, framed by cardón cacti of magnificent heights and cartoonish shapes.

Were they two sizes too big, or was I two sizes too small? I'd fallen down my own version of Alice's rabbit hole long ago, so either was feasible.

I could see a set of tire tracks in the sand, which was always a welcome sight, given that I had no cell service whatsoever and could scarcely get my location to show up on any of my map apps. I'd refresh and refresh, but the little blue dot that represented me always remained suspended in the center of the screen amid blank latitude and longitude lines. As if I really was nowhere at all.

And so it was all trial and error... day after day, dirt road after dead end, after dirt road, after dead end, until you find one that *actually* goes somewhere. I knew which direction the Sea of Cortés was purely because I could see the tip of a rocky island jutting up *just* above the horizon.

It looked like this particular road was heading straight toward it. Not to mention, the single pair of existing tire tracks meant that at least one other person thought it was a place worth going, even if it was just a local doing a poor job at rounding up his cows.

The sand beneath the tires was so smooth that, for the first few miles, it felt more like driving a boat. We floated along beneath the piercing blue sky, green yucca and red-flowering barrel cacti like buoys on either side guiding our course.

The dogs' tongues flapped out of each and every open window, because despite it being in the mid-nineties, I still had them all open. Even the sunroof. I was always comforted by the heaviness of the heat, as if it was the only thing keeping me firmly tethered to the ground when I stepped out of the car.

The tracks I'd been following ended abruptly in a three-point turn where the sand started to get much deeper and much softer. So much so that I could see the detail of the tire treads in the impression they had left. I stood beside them to compare their width to my own tires, which were big-ass thirty-fives that had yet to fail me. The dogs whined as I stood with my hands on my hips. "The sand is wayyyyy too hot for you guys right here," I yelled back over the running engine.

"But I got a good feeling about this one!" I exclaimed as I made my way around the Jeep from tire to tire, letting some air out for optimal sand travel. This is a trick I learned only after damn near burying Bertha on the ever-shifting shores of Lake Powell. An older couple on an ATV had driven over to dole out this helpful advice (and bring me a cold beer for my troubles). But they didn't hover; they didn't even stay more than a few minutes before wishing me luck and disappearing back over the dunes. I remember being thrilled that they assumed I could get myself out. Because I did.

The giant cardóns and saguaros gave way to ocotillo and spiky cholla cacti that stretched out far more horizontally than vertically. The sand continued to deepen as more and more bleached white shells glittered in the sun around us. We were close.

With the remaining flora only about thigh-high, I could see farther in each direction. I could also see now that I was no longer on a road at all.

I had hoped we could make it all the way to the water's edge, but by the time I could smell the salt, I was essentially plowing the sand instead of driving over it. The tires could go no farther. I stepped out barefoot to test how hot it was before releasing the hounds. I was thrilled to find that the winds off the bay made things considerably cooler.

The final dune was gradual, but tall. There were patches of seagrass swaying at the top. Whatever we were looking for if it existed was just over that hill.

I loved that the dogs were faster than me, that they always got there first. I watched the wind hit their ears as they stood all in a row looking out at what I couldn't yet see. By the time I crested the top of the dune, there were four perfect trails of pawprints through the spotless sand, straight into the turquoise water.

I squinted to my right and then to my left. It was only a few days from August, which has an average high of one hundred degrees, so it was no surprise that the beaches were abandoned. I used my phone to zoom in on the closest thing I could see, which ended up being a red sunshade, beneath which sat one single fisherman, his pole anchored in the sand in front of him, line straight out into the sea.

Other than that, it was nothing but me and the dogs and the white sand beside blue sea beneath cloudless sky.

Dagwood stood at the water's edge, letting it lap against his front legs as he looked back toward me, slack-jawed and smiling. Bucket had started swimming out toward two pelicans bobbing on the surf. Birdie followed her frantically while Banjo dug at the hermit crabs bubbling up through the damp sand.

The tide was perfect. Not too high, not too low. I walked backward along the waterline, watching our five sets of prints dissolve after each wave, sweeping away any evidence that we were ever there at all.

The sun was nearly setting by the time I backed the Jeep precariously through the same tracks I'd made on the way in. The dogs were asleep in a content, exhausted pile, their limbs rocking loosely over the ruts in the road. The cacti all turned to silhouettes against a deeply pink sky. Behind me, a dark blue and the flickering of the first stars.

It was (and remains to this day) one of the best days I've ever had. The kind that you hope you wake up in if there's anything after this life. And all I thought about as I stared out over the wheel ... was how excited I was to tell William about it.

The following day, I was scheduled to start heading back north. Mind you, anything I had "scheduled" was just some imaginary thing I did to mimic what felt like adulthood. The reality was, I did not have to be anywhere at any time. I could head north, south, east, west, or straight into the Pacific for all anyone cared.

But since my journey north was taking me through a bigger city, I thought the Wi-Fi might be halfway decent. At least, I hoped it would, given that William and I were going to try to FaceTime that night.

It felt like ... a date. And this is where it warrants reminding that the last time I went on a "first date," I was a teenager.

"Did he say it like ... like a *date* date?" my mom wondered aloud via speakerphone on the bathroom sink beside me.

"I don't know. If it's at a scheduled time, isn't that a date?!" I snapped.

She knew I was nervous. And I *hated* that I was nervous.

I had spent five full minutes trying to decide what was the most normal way to sit by the time his face came to life on my screen. I'd forgotten how deep his voice was. He was wearing a faded brown linen shirt, loosely holding a tumbler of whiskey with a hand covered in turquoise rings.

He was one of the *manliest* men I'd ever met. He was a competitive rugby player and a mountaineer and a fisherman and a bow hunter. He took his first deer at just nine years old. You know . . . *man* stuff. And yet, he also collected turquoise rings and painted his toes every now and again just for fun. His best friend is a famous drag queen. His paradoxes were familiar, disarming in a way. I was pretty taken with him, so impulsively I started to do what my therapist calls "stomping the ice."

I recounted the most outrageous stories, told the most self-deprecating jokes, spoke openly about my divorce without shrouding some of the anger that still lingered, and—of course—swore like a sailor all the while.

I had *stomped stomped stomped*, and now it was time to take a step back, hold my breath, and see if the ice broke . . . see if the weight of who I was at my absolute *most* was too much to hold. Better to find out right away as opposed to waiting a whole decade, only to be plunged suddenly—violently—into the cold, all because you couldn't hear the delicate splintering beneath your feet.

When I finally stopped to take a breath, he took a swig of his whiskey and smiled at me; the light from the lantern in his yurt flashing across his piercing blue eyes.

"You swear a lot."

A week later, I stood over the lone kitchen pot, boiling water for one of the instant coffee packets that seemed to come standard with every Airbnb I had stayed in.

As I stirred in the sugar, I found myself smiling, thinking about how William teased my pronunciation of *coffee*. I could have sworn

I'd been gone from the East Coast long enough to not say "caaw-fee," but his Midwestern ear had caught what little remained.

Meanwhile, I had found it highly entertaining that he said "pop" instead of soda. He couldn't believe I said "soda" instead of pop. We covered a lot of colloquialisms, but as I drove north on Route 1 toward the US border, I found myself wondering if he called it the "highway" or the "freeway."

Where I grew up, most folks called it "the highway," so naturally I did too. It was an awful, crowded thing that seemed to induce an unparalleled rage in its users. Only when I moved out west did I start calling it "the *free*way." That made a whole lot more sense out here.

Regardless of what you call it, I rode it from sunup to sundown for the next four days, barreling toward Utah through the thick August heat.

The sun was setting on my final stretch, soaking everything in its last light as I drove up through San Felipe toward the border. A folk band plucked their mandolins through my car stereo, up and out the windows into the dusk.

I tried to bite my lip to keep the smile from spreading across my face. William was catching a flight to Utah the following day.

I'll be waiting for you when you get there, he wrote.

Our two blue dots were making their way across the grid toward each other.

chapter seven

Trailer for Two

It's strange to feel like you might be in love with someone when you've never even kissed them. Strange for me, at least, as I thought that kind of thing was reserved for the devoutly religious. Technically, we had spent less than four hours together. *Technologically,* much more. But it still feels odd to be nervous to "meet" someone you already know well enough to "love."

I wasn't just out of my comfort zone; I was completely out of its orbit at this point. When he texted to say he'd landed, I felt sick to my stomach, as excitement and complete panic battled it out. Fortunately, he had landed in Salt Lake City so he could pick up Ruby (his van) that he'd left at a friend's place.

That meant he was still three and a half hours away, which would give me three and a half hours to get my fucking shit together.

When I left for Baja, I threw everything into the trailer in one giant pile on the floor. Lawn chairs, dog beds, water jugs, power tools. I *was* planning to leave it in better shape, but it started raining like it always does on an afternoon in July, so half of the things were cleanish, and the other half had dragged in *quite* a mess.

Fortunately, it's so damn dry out there that any wet sand or dirt just returns to its original form and blows off with a few good shakes. There's rarely any real "mud" (unless there's been a flash flood, of course; that's the *best* toe-squishing mud), and there's no humidity so the dogs don't ever have that musty smell to their fur. I'd wager to say that between the four of them, I've doled out less than fifteen baths total in the past decade-plus. That's what the river is for.

This was all going to come in handy since I had arrived late the night before, opened the trailer, crawled over that pile to my mattress, and passed out cold.

Now I had three and a half hours to make this place look . . . acceptable.

In the world I grew up in, *living* in a *trailer* was one of the most "low-class," embarrassing things one could imagine.

We would play this game in grade school where you'd write down a list of boys in class (say, Tommy, Billy, Robby), a list of jobs (nurse, model, mom), number of kids (two, four, ten, and something crazy, like fifty), and kinds of houses (apartment, mansion, house, trailer).

I will say it was kind of progressive of us to list *mom* as a job, though, because it *absolutely* is. That's why I've never applied.

Each girl would pick a number or roll dice ... or something, I don't know—it was, like, twenty-five years ago. The numbers you picked would *reveal your future*.

"Your turn, Brianna!" they would say.

We'd all hold our breath as the results came in.

"Okay ... you are going to marry Robby." A chorus of *oohs* and *aahs*. "And you're gonna be a nurse who lives in a *trailer* with four kids!!!!!" An eruption of laughter. It didn't get worse than that.

Later on, in high school, it was tradition for us girls to attend the Friday night football games and stand in the bleachers in Ugg boots and teeny-tiny denim Abercrombie miniskirts. Fairfield Prep was sort of the unofficial "brother school" to my all-girls "academy." We were the *private-school* kids. Lauralton girls always, always dated Prep guys, and going to a party at a *public-school kid's* house? What are you, some sort of delinquent?!

Present at every Friday night football game was a swath of (designated) bleachers packed with shirtless high school boys with painted faces, chanting and jeering out at the field. They called themselves "the Bomb Squad." Everyone who was anyone was there, and if you didn't know the cheers, it was a big faux pas.

Whenever the opposing team was from a public school (especially one from a city like the one I lived in) they pulled out one of their classics. Some drunk, red-faced senior would scream, "WHEELS ON THE BUS!!!!" so we all knew what was coming.

Then we'd erupt in song, all our fingers pointing accusatorily at the opposite bleachers.

Theee wheels on your HOUSE go round and round, round and

round, round and round, the wheels on your HOUSE go round and round, aallll through the town!!!

Then we'd all high-five triumphantly, because we didn't live in *trailers* like those *public-school kids*. As if any of us had one single thing to do with the amount of money our parents had, or didn't have.

Mary Karr's late father summed it up beautifully when he reminded her throughout her life that there are some folks "born on third base thinking they hit a triple."

Classroom jeers and high school chants echoed in my head as I stood barefoot in my dirt driveway. *Ew, you live in a TRAILER with four kids!!!*

The thing now, of course, is that I did not give one single fuck. I loved my trailer. It had thus far been my favorite place I'd ever lived, second only to Bertha. And I actually used to sing the "wheels on your house" bit every now and again when I was driving her along some sun-soaked freeway, free from anyone else's definitive opinion on what wealth truly is.

Now, it should be stated that of course I can't *actually* remember what answers I got, or how many hundreds of variations of futures I was shown in the back of the school bus over the years, but I like to think there's a good chance that at *some* point... I had been destined to live in a trailer with four kids. They just turned out to be the kind with fur.

And that fur was *everywhere*. Though I couldn't imagine William would be surprised since he had already seen my car. Regardless, I grabbed a leaf blower and aimed it directly into the trailer door, watching tumbleweeds of dog hair swirl up into the air, along with the dried sand and dirt from the once-wet lawn chairs.

The trick was to get all the sand and fur up off the floor and then quickly change the angle of the airflow to send it all right out the windows. I stood there satisfied for a minute or two before at least a quarter of it floated back down, coating every surface just a *little* less than before. Futile.

Stepping out onto the deck, I scanned the yard (a.k.a. the dirt clearing at the top of the driveway in which my trailer sat). Other than a dozen or more fossilized dog toys, it was looking pretty good.

I swept off the stone path that led out to my lounge chair, rearranging the twisted dead juniper branches I'd used to line it along the way. Banjo and Bucket spent every morning digging beneath them on the hunt for lizards, no matter how many times I asked them to pick *any* other branches on the entire nine acres. Fortunately, most of the bigger ones were cemented into the ground after a year's worth of storms had sent thick mud seeping into every crevice around them.

Bertha was in her resting place on the far left of the yard, where the floods had cemented in her tires too. She was my favorite part of the landscape.

Back inside the trailer, I wiped the countertops and put on a fresh pair of sheets. Things were looking good. *Realistic,* but good. I didn't want this guy thinking I was Martha fucking Stewart. Although, that was probably evident from the moment we met.

Around the back of the trailer was a whole different story. Martha would have passed out.

There was a pile of warped, sun-faded scraps of wood that had once been the *first* lounge chair I'd brought up here.

The constant beating of the sun and relentless summer heat had dried it to within an inch of its life. One day I looked out the window after a rainstorm to find it had cracked in half entirely. I had meant to burn it, but I must have come up with something better to do.

Leaning against one of the larger juniper trees were a few rusted bike racks that I had in the back of Bertha, along with a big gray garbage can being held in place by a stack of cement blocks that I sometimes used to reinforce the trailer tires.

Leaning up against another juniper tree was one of those industrial-looking patio heaters they use at bars and restaurants. I'd bought it the winter before, but yet another storm had blown through with winds strong enough to tip it over, despite having a half-full tank of propane inside. It stood there now with the top portion cracked off and hanging limply, connected only by a few cables and wires as if someone had attempted to behead it. Between two junipers, I'd strung up a clothesline of dog lifejackets.

There was also the obligatory pile of rebar, and a bucket full of dishes I had yet to take to the car wash.

People who live in trailers get a bad rap, but the stuff out on our lawns is scarcely different from the stuff in other folks' basements and garages. If we *had* those, I bet a lot of us *would* put our stuff in there. I know I would. But all I had was dirt.

The pathetically flimsy shed I had nearly died trying to assemble earlier that year had succumbed to a particularly vicious flood that ripped the earth out from underneath it, causing the floor to shift and the walls to collapse inward like a teepee.

It did say *quite clearly* on the box to ONLY BUILD ON A FLAT CEMENT SURFACE, so I had nobody to blame but me.

It was a storm I'm glad the dogs and I weren't up there for. We'd been down in New Mexico traipsing around on blinding white sand dunes as far as the eye could see. I was grateful, however, that the way the shed had fallen still served as . . . let's call it "decent" protection for the things I had inside.

So, naturally, I just shrugged and left it like that.

Before I went to Baja, however, I *had* gotten around to breaking everything down and stacking the mangled plastic pieces in a huge pile. If I had a pickup truck or was willing to ask anyone for help with *anything*, I could have had it all out of there after a few runs to the dump. But all I had was my tiny little rock-crawling Jeep, packed to the brim with dogs that I couldn't leave in the trailer without air-conditioning. I couldn't leave them anywhere, in fact, because I'd lost the ability to function without them.

Even if they hadn't been in the back, the walls of the shed were nearly the same width as the Jeep itself. I couldn't fit a single one of the aforementioned piles in there, so I just shrugged and left those laying around too.

None of these things were things I thought about. Those damn floods give everything enough of a desert patina that even the garbage looks like it fits somehow. Plus, I was too busy doing nothing.

I had canyons to see, rivers to float, dogs to run off with. The mess didn't bother me, and it sure as hell didn't bother them.

They most certainly contributed to the making of it, after all.

By the time William's maroon Volkswagen Vanagon crept up the driveway, I had come to terms with the state of my little junkyard. If he didn't like it, he could back right down and go regale Reddit with "behind-the-scenes" tales of my ramshackle setup.

I shook my head, trying to snap myself out of the paranoia that still held on to the coattails of my every thought.

I could see his smile through the windshield as a little hula girl bobblehead shook side to side on the dashboard. There was a bouquet of wild turkey feathers tucked beneath the passenger side visor. The dogs crowded around excitedly when he stepped out of the van, which gave me a moment to figure out if I should try to kiss him? *Was he going to try to kiss me?* I went in for a hug immediately, just to be safe.

"Hey, guyss!!" he said, excitedly, reaching down to pet the dogs competing for his attention. "Nice to see you all again!"

I watched his eyes bounce from me to trailer to dog to deck to another dog to the piles behind the trailer. In an attempt to avoid eye contact, I immediately offered a tour of the property. My breathing slowed as we set off through the sagebrush over toward the northeast corner that I call the Caves.

To get there, you have to follow one of the many narrow washes that snake down from the rock wall all the way to the front of the property. Water carves trails through the desert better than any human ever could.

He walked behind me as I chattered on about how old the junipers were, and the names of the different kinds of sandstone.

"Right here!" I exclaimed, pointing to a nondescript patch of dirt. "Right here is where the first Indian paintbrush flowers pop up. I've got a lot of flowering prickly pears, and one little barrel cactus down by the big wash, but I didn't know if I'd ever get th—"

He put his hands on my shoulders and gently turned me toward him. This was the closest I'd ever been to his eyes. They were the same blue as the Sea of Cortés. Then he placed his hands on my cheeks, leaned down, and kissed me.

The next few days were much of the same. We'd lay in the sun reading, sneak off behind some rock somewhere, stay up late talking by candlelight. One night he gave me a stick-and-poke tattoo of the little dipper on my shoulder; then we laid side by side on the deck staring up at it, buzzed on boxed wine and newness. The sheer size of him was more apparent than ever when he was inside the trailer. The top of his head was flush against the ceiling, so we spent most of our time outside, which was how the dogs and I spent most of our time anyway.

I would have gone around and introduced him to my friends if I'd had any. The only people I could think to "introduce" him to were the handful of folks I spoke to a few times a week, like Alex, the gas station manager who always brought treats out to the dogs when he filled my propane tanks.

Or Harry and Drew, who owned the little coffee drive-thru I'd treat myself to every now and again. They knew my order by heart.

They *also* knew to have dog treats on hand the moment they saw my car.

"Still got four in there?!" they'd say.

Once, when I was fostering a litter from the shelter, I pulled up with a pile of puppies strewn across the front seat, the center console, and my lap.

"I've got eleven today, guys, so you can hold the treats," I laughed. (They gave me eleven anyway.) I used to joke that we cleaned out the whole town by the time our errands were done.

I never did ask her name, but there was a cashier at the Walker Drug with long gray braids and a pack-a-day voice who always called me "hon." I suspected she probably called everyone that, but one day, as I stood in a long, peak-tourist-season line with handfuls of screws and hooks, I watched her greet each customer. I waited for her to say it, but she never did.

When I got up to the counter, she glanced up from the clacking of the cash register, and smiled. "Hey, hon!!"

The owner of my storage unit in town was another character. The first time I went to his office, it was covered wall to wall, floor to ceiling with books. In order to take down my information to rent me the unit, he had to clear even more books from on top of his desk. When he found out I was a writer, we sat and talked for almost an hour.

To this day, he still texts me book recommendations.

And, of course, there was a lady I called "my rat dealer." She lived in a trailer next to a small dirt-bike park and had a basement full of reptiles and a closet full of rats to feed to them. I'd shoot her a text every few weeks to go pick some up to feed Bean and Mae. (It is a horrific, necessary, awful thing to have to do this. I wish snakes ate salad, but they do not. They eat rats.)

When the weather started cooling off at night, I knew I needed to find a safer place for my snakes to stay. They needed a constant heat source, which in the winter, I could not provide without working outlets. I asked my rat dealer if she could temporarily house them in her basement with all of *her* snakes. She agreed, and as a gesture of goodwill, I sent her thirty dollars a month on Venmo, labeled "snake rent." That was the first and only form of rent I'd paid in *years*.

Harry, Drew, Mike from storage, my rat dealer, and a random (albeit lovely) cashier . . . that was the extent of my "community." I wonder if they ever even considered what their small, repetitive kindnesses meant to me during a time when I was convinced the whole world was out to get me.

For a few fleeting moments each week, they made me feel normal. They reminded me that I still existed. That I wasn't just a ghost up on the hill.

I might not have had anyone prominent to introduce William to, but I had about a hundred different dirt roads waiting for us with open arms.

On a particularly warm day that fall, I drove us up through a wall of sandstone fins to a creek that ran along the back side of it. By that time of year, it was down to a trickle, and the only place to access what was left of the water was, quite literally, the middle of the road.

The creek flowed over the top of it, serving as a fun little obstacle to floor your ATVs and dirt bikes through, but to most people, there was nothing overtly special about a little bit of water flowing over a dirt road.

The dogs leapt out of the Jeep and darted off toward the same place they'd been digging for something the last time we'd been there. I kicked off my flip-flops and waded into the knee-deep puddle, spinning around with my arms out.

"Isn't this great?!" I exclaimed. "I hardly *ever* see anyone back here."

If you recall, that is my benchmark for whether or not somewhere is worth going.

William, on the other hand, was a professional photographer. His passion *and* his livelihood were based on the epic views, the iconic sunsets, the legendary mountaintops, the best campsites, the most desirable travel destinations. And those are usually *very* crowded and *not* dog-friendly. At least, not for *my* dogs.

By the time William came for that first visit, Banjo was eight months old and had never been on a leash. He was raised, from birth, out here on these dirt roads, drinking from these muddy puddles, rolling in some dead carcass, happy as a pig in shit.

We were lounging on the flat red rocks beside the water when he wriggled his way up in between the two of us and shook off, showering us in cold river water that actually felt wonderful on such a warm afternoon.

When it came to sleeping arrangements, we ran into another size-related problem. My bed in the corner of the trailer was a built-in, full-size mattress, which had been plenty roomy for a gal and four dogs who've spent many nights sleeping in the back of a Jeep Wrangler without issue. Not to mention, Dagwood always jumped off the bed shortly after I'd fallen asleep and spent the rest of the night on the couch in front of the screen door, keeping watch.

I, myself, am not exactly a small person either. Five foot ten, in fact, and the frizz on top of my blond curls visually adds another inch at least. *And*, as those pin-dick high schoolers never failed to point out, I have a broad set of shoulders on me. With William's six-foot-five-on-a-good-day frame, there was hardly room for the two of us, let alone *six* of us.

I'm sure he thought it was strange that I teared up when we climbed into bed together the very first night. Not because I was with *a new man* . . . but because of how the dogs stood beside the bed, looking up, wondering where *they* were going to fit. Realistically, they just . . . weren't.

It was devastating. So devastating, in fact, that I *actually* considered asking him to sleep in his van. Instead, he watched silently as I snapped the couch down into futon mode, making a nest of pillows and blankets, tucking them each in delicately with a kiss on the forehead.

I backed up slowly toward the bed, fighting back tears, whispering, "Stay, I love you, good night." In that moment, I didn't care what William thought. This would be the first night in years that I hadn't slept in bed with my dogs.

When I finally lay down, I sighed deeply, resting my head on his bare chest. He rubbed my back gently, and whispered, "Tell me again how you picked all of their names . . ."

homesick nomad

. . .

The next morning, William stayed back at the trailer to boil water for coffee while I strolled the grounds with the dogs. "Don't worry," I whispered, "he's leaving on Tuesday."

Long before we met, he had planned a trip to raft down the Grand Canyon for an entire month. He would have no way to communicate outside of a satellite phone reserved for emergencies.

Just as quickly as he was there, he was gone.

The dogs happily piled into the bed that night, and I sighed a breath of relief at the return to normalcy, at the soft shapes of their bodies melding in with mine. Days went by, and I found myself thinking of him often, but cautiously. I wouldn't allow myself to wonder if he was thinking about me, because both potential answers were equally nerve-racking.

Maybe this had just been some torrid, temporary love affair. Maybe a few days was all it took to get out of each other's systems.

After two weeks, my life felt exactly like it had before. My phone scarcely buzzed. I didn't even bother scaling up the back wall of my property on the prayer of catching a single, fleeting bar of service. It was just the dogs and me, back out on My Beach, leaving only our footprints.

On the way back to the trailer one afternoon after lolling about beside the river all morning, I stopped by the post office to check my mailbox. (The local government says you have to have a *house* at your address in order to get a real mailbox. The trailer discrimination continues.)

Inside were a few envelopes, a pamphlet about an upcoming local election, and a little brown box tied with a white ribbon. I carried it over to the counter and unwrapped it gently. Inside was a pair of turquoise earrings and a note.

> By the time you get this, I will have been on the river for a while. Just know I'll be thinking of you.
>
> Xx William

He'd asked his silversmith friend to make them for me . . . to mail them only after he'd been gone awhile.

The following week, another letter came, postmarked from Phantom Ranch with a big red stamp that said MAILED BY MULE FROM THE BOTTOM OF THE GRAND CANYON.

I taped the envelope to my nonfunctioning fridge. Then I taped the note from the jewelry box beside it.

I don't know at what point we started calling each other "boyfriend" and "girlfriend," because frankly, it felt like we were a little too old for that. But just a few weeks after he got off the river, we decided to go to Baja together for the whole winter, so that felt . . . pretty serious, whether we had some sort of official title or not.

I was nervous at first, and still riding the high of my solo trip down there just a few months earlier. But after all the years I'd spent

homesick nomad

dreaming of cruising down the Baja peninsula, I was thrilled to be able to say that I had now gone twice in less than six months.

We spent a few weeks camping with friends celebrating Christmas around a beach bonfire, over whatever fresh catch William brought in from an afternoon of spearfishing in his slick, black wet suit that made him look like James Bond emerging from the ocean. After dinner, we'd play card games beneath the twinkling lights and embroidered stockings hanging from our cars.

After Christmas, it was just the four dogs and the two of us, bouncing from beach to beach, taco truck to taco truck, and a few Airbnbs for special occasions.

For my birthday in mid-January, William booked us a bright orange stucco house that overlooked the Bahía Concepción, famous for the gray whales that time of year. "Look! Look!" we'd shout, pointing out toward their telltale sprays on the horizon. The views were breathtaking, but the home itself was simple. I recall being extremely grateful for the lack of floor rugs when Banjo started having uncontrollable diarrhea from one end of the house to the other.

The morning of my birthday was spent using Google Translate to communicate with a veterinarian who gave us some antibiotics and electrolyte packets for Banjo's water. It was essentially Gatorade for dogs, which is fitting given that the powder made the water glow a color that could certainly be described as lemon-lime.

That evening, William pulled out a bag of tiny plastic dinosaur figurines he had found at a gas station and used them to decorate the top of a single-layer birthday cake we'd made with a powdered mix (also from the gas station).

Banjo was feeling better, but there was still some . . . leakage, let's call it, so William carried him off toward the bathroom while I piled dishes into the sink. I could hear him saying something to Banjo, but it was muffled by the sound of water filling the tub.

I was struggling to open one of the electrolyte packets when they returned a short while later. Banjo was wrapped in a towel, his head bouncing gently on William's shoulder with each step he took. It looked like he was holding a sleeping baby after a long day at the beach.

When tearing at the plastic packet proved futile, I started biting at the corner of it with my teeth, before rummaging through the sparsely supplied drawers for a pair of scissors, talking aloud to no one in particular about lord knows what.

Reluctantly, I turned to ask William for help, but he was already down on one knee with a question of his own.

When I saw him kneeling there with a turquoise ring, I should have been shocked, maybe even scared. We had only known each other for five months at that point, and had been physically in the same location for less than half of that time.

But the way he chose to ask me, there on the kitchen floor, eye level with a bunch of dogs, one of whose butt fur he had just scrubbed for the fifth time that day . . . it felt *real*.

I'm sure it sounds self-deprecating in a way, but when I looked down at that man, I saw someone who knew *exactly* what they were signing up for.

chapter eight

Where To

I knew from the moment we met that William and I were *very* different. I loved the desert; he loved the mountains. He was tremendously organized; I was a train wreck. I had four dogs; he had no dogs.

He'd never been married, never had children, never even had a pet since he left the family farm. Instead, he'd spent the better part of a decade traveling the world, sailing to Hawaii, backpacking across New Zealand, kayaking off the coast of Portugal, shooting photos of the famous cellist Yo-Yo Ma on a glacier in Alaska . . .

As for me, when I wasn't at my trailer in Moab, I was in Arizona or New Mexico or Baja, or on monthslong book tours in a smattering of Airbnbs and seedy motels throughout the country with four dogs in tow.

We were both fiercely independent and always on the road. Our stories, regardless of how different, were our most profound similarity. We had lived lives worth telling about.

But it wasn't until I was on the way back from Baja with a ring on my finger that I realized we hadn't exactly talked about what was next . . . about how we were going to combine two totally different plotlines into the same story.

William still only had Ruby to call a home, and my trailer wasn't exactly equipped for late winter up on the mesa. I had no problem handling three-digit temperatures, but anything below fifty degrees was practically unbearable to me, especially because the trailer had no viable heat source. I casually mentioned to William that I'd been heating it up the previous winter by turning the little stove on and propping it open.

He was horrified, to which I protested that I *always* turned it off before bed, and only got up to turn it back on around 3 a.m., when the chill set in enough to creep beneath the covers. That did nothing to comfort him.

He, on the other hand, *loved* the cold. He loved the cold and backcountry skiing and mountaineering and fly-fishing in thigh-deep water in the dead of winter.

He loved audiobooks and wanted to play them nonstop the entire drive back up from Baja, but I *have* to listen to music, otherwise my own books won't get written.

"What??" He laughed, looking over at me from behind the wheel.

I explained that I do all my best thinking when I'm driving with the windows down and the music up. Sometimes a particular song lyric drifts from the speaker as the sun is hitting the windshield just right, and you suddenly remember something you'd nearly forgotten.

Somewhere along our way north, we decided that it made the most sense to just go back to the trailer, though we did toss around the idea of renting an Airbnb somewhere for a month or two.

"I'm sure I can figure out a heating situation for us," he said confidently.

The following week, he stood over the user manual that had come with the trailer. It too was from the 1980s, so it was stained a sort of urine color and smelled like a library. I'd never bothered to open it, which he was absolutely confounded by. Especially when he put the pages down a few minutes later, walked over to a switch that I'd never really noticed before, and flicked it up and down a couple times.

On the final upward flick, a whining sound rattled the entire trailer as dust (probably also from the 1980s) flew out of a handful of small vents around the baseboards.

"Did you just . . ." I stared incredulously.

It took a few minutes before the air filling the trailer turned from cold and dusty to hot and dusty. We both choked on the burning smell as the whining got louder and louder. Eventually, we thought it best to shut it back off.

I sat outside on the deck beneath a blanket as the dogs crunched around on the frozen ground. William was inside on all fours, spreading out various manual pages, using my tools to unscrew the vent covers. After a good twenty minutes or so, I stood up to linger in the doorway.

"If you really don't want to use the stove method, we can just get one of those Little Buddy brand propane heaters with the carbon monoxide alarm on it," I offered.

"I'm pretty sure I can fix it, baby," he said, with half his head still inside the vent. I never thought I would be the type who liked being called "baby," but there was just something about the way it rolled off his tongue...

I stomped back to my camp chair on the deck and sat down with a heavy sigh. I hated that he was *fixing* things, because it felt like an attempt to *fix* me. I liked the way my life worked, even the things that didn't work at all. I didn't need all that fluff. The way I lived was fine by me. But since I had just agreed to *share* my life with this person, I figured I should get used to the idea that he might have a say in it.

Over the next month, William continued to busy himself with a different project every day. Banjo and Birdie would sit diligently beside him as he lay sprawled out beneath the trailer, banging pipes around and looking for loose connections.

The last time I'd been under there, I was using some infomercial glue gun to finally seal up the holding tank for the toilet. I'd gone months and months without it, but even when it was working again, I still chose to pee outside, even in the cold. Two to three in the morning is the best time to see the stars. How could I be expected to miss that?

Next, he set up a big wall of solar panels and ordered a special hookup that would allow us to plug directly into the massive power bank that was being charged by said panels.

"Wait for itttttt . . ." he said excitedly when I got back from watching an early winter sunset with the dogs.

He walked from one end of the trailer to the other (a.k.a. five steps), clicking little buttons above him, filling it with a yellowish, flickering glow from the antique ceiling lights. You could see the bodies of a few long-dead moths preserved inside the glass.

"Wow, I can't believe it," I said half-heartedly.

After a dinner of canned soup and boxed wine, I insisted that we turn them all off and light the candles instead.

Before William moved up to the property, I had prided myself on being able to withstand discomfort. But he was perplexed as to why I consistently did *nothing* to improve what were . . . pretty easily improvable situations.

It wasn't like any of these were wildly expensive fixes, or labor-intensive endeavors. Fuck's sake, all he had to do to figure out the heat was read a page from the manual and flip a switch. Even if that switch didn't quite work *or* produce the nicest sound, it was still something I'd never considered.

It was quite like when my best friend, Mary, came out to visit me in 2020 and spent half the trip begging me to just fix that damn toilet. It seemed so obvious to her, to anyone who hadn't sunk all the way into the sands of this strange world I'd made.

I couldn't explain it to Mary then, and I certainly didn't know how to explain it to William now for fear that I would just compulsively blurt out, "Can't you just let me be messy and impractical?! Can't you just let me struggle?"

Weird hill to die on, I know, but his attempts to make life easier for me felt more like he was trying to *save* me . . . like he had no idea how I had survived until he came along to bestow light and heat and working outlets and a pair of arms to fall asleep in at night.

I didn't want his help. In fact, I was *offended* by it. For the first time in a long time, it was purely someone's company I was after. I could have figured out how to do all of those things; I just never bothered to because I told myself that I couldn't get *soft*. I needed to prove that I could tough it out.

That I could live in a metal box in one-hundred-degree weather. If it got too hot, I'd just crawl underneath it into the cool dirt with the dogs or go hide out beneath the river water until the sun began to sink.

That I could sit calmly while gnats and blackflies buzzed all around me, while beetles and spiders crawled across my legs in the middle of the night because Banjo busted out both screens on the windows above the bed.

I didn't need running water, because I'd just lift up multiple five-gallon jugs of lukewarm water all day, every day to distribute between my cup and the dogs' bowl. How else would I get my arm workouts in?

And while five bucks at the community pool in town got me access to a shower stall with a dispenser of surprisingly nice cranberry-orange soap, I much preferred heating up some water in a pot and scrubbing my naked body down on the porch. The warped wood retained so much heat from the afternoon sun that it felt like standing in a sauna. I never even needed a towel.

I'm sure it sounds like I'd become some sort of doomsday prepper, ready to tough out every extreme, ready to live in a cave and eat whatever the dogs brought back for us. The truth is, I'd just learned that being adaptable was the safest thing to be.

Regardless, what plenty of folks might consider "rock bottom" was perfectly comfortable to me. When you end up a proud prototype of the famous Chris Farley *livin' in a van down by the river* skit on *Saturday Night Live*, you can assume your standards differ slightly from your average American dreamer's. Statistically, I think most people would feel quite destitute if they suddenly had to live in their car. But there was a sense of security in knowing that other peoples' lows were highs to me.

Change is one of the few and most formidable constants in this life. That's why ease can come at a cost. When things become mindless, you stop paying attention. Your willingness to change course or shift perspective dwindles. You grow so accustomed to comforts that you mistake them for necessities. You forget what you're capable of.

So many people end up staying in unhappy lives because going down amid the soothing familiarity of your doomed ship feels like the only option if you've forgotten that you know how to swim.

When William went away for a photoshoot the following week, the dogs and I were on our own again for a good while.

I left dishes in the sink and shaved my legs in a bucket on the front porch with a cigarette poised between my lips and Lainey Wilson on the speaker up loud. I never turned the lights on or plugged anything into the outlets. I peed outside every night, the cold air nipping at my bare butt while I stared up at the Milky Way as it split the whole night sky in half.

When the dogs stayed out wandering a little too late, I was stubborn enough to keep carrying a battery-powered lantern through the dark, hunched over and wrapped in a shawl like an old witch. The *much* more effective flashlight William had put in the trailer sat untouched in the drawer where he'd left it.

I'd been finding my own way through the dark for a long time by then. As long as I could remember in fact.

I was only eleven when my father went to rehab. Sixteen when he left for good. My brother moved out to Montana shortly after he and my mom walked in on my father having an affair. It was up to me to be my mother's protector.

Sometimes I wish my dad had left when I was small... too small for me to remember how he threw his head back when he laughed. How he always had a slight shake to his hands. How he tucked my tiny body between his legs and made a pizza the whole way down the ski slope.

He was an alcoholic, but sometimes I wish he'd been an awful one. A horrible screaming drunk instead of the silly, affectionate, earnest father that he'd been. If my memories were filled with shouting matches and shattering glass, perhaps my brain might actually try to protect me from them. Instead, in all of the flashbacks of my father, I feel safe. It feels like everything glows.

So, my brain plays the old film roll in my head over and over and over and in a cruel twist, it only grows more alluring with time. The mundane becomes extraordinary; a historical moment preserved in a frame in a sparsely decorated hall. Because it's been more than half my life since there was anything new to hang there.

How can you not cling to something if it's the only thing you have left? How can you avoid the survival instinct to romanticize every last inch of what you'll never have again?

I could never figure out how to make that hurt less. Even after all these years, I still haven't. It still felt like a fresh wound, made only deeper by Neil slipping so suddenly into the very same darkness. It's as if he was there one day and gone the next.

My divorce caught me just as off guard as my parents' had.

When William and I first met, I was still bouncing between total disassociation and hypervigilance. I would not be fooled a third time. My head could not, *would not*, wrap itself around what I knew my heart was feeling, so I spent the early days of our relationship keeping more distance than he even knew.

I didn't want to get close enough to confirm what I feared the most. That maybe the way my marriage ended had mixed in with my father's abandonment, creating some perfect witch's potion that rendered me incapable of *really* falling in love (with a human, that is). Because real love requires trust. And no one had made me a potion for that.

When William got back from his photoshoot, he came equipped with a list of houses that his Realtor had sent him.

Your Realtor?! I shouted (only in my head) because within seconds I remembered that he had started talking with real estate agents before we'd even met. I'm sure he'd mentioned it several times since, but it's easy to miss things when you spend most of your time scanning your surroundings, plotting an escape if the need for one should arise.

I had spoken with *one* Realtor *one* time after she showed me *one* listing, which was the property that I bought, so I didn't have much worthwhile input.

My property was just a patch of totally undeveloped desert, so I couldn't *imagine* the ins and outs of buying a whole entire house. (This is one of *many* ways in which it feels like I stopped "growing up" at some point. Or maybe "maturing" is the correct word. Regardless, I had never been interested in either, so that's fine. But it's hard not to reckon with it when you're completely overwhelmed by mundane things that make perfect sense to other folks your age. Nowadays, at thirty-five, when someone tells me they're pregnant, I *still* have that knee-jerk reaction, that internal gasp reminiscent of finding out your high school friend got knocked up after prom—but we'll talk more about that later.)

William and I sat side by side on the deck as he scrolled through photos. I was more than happy to help him look. Mainly because it felt like it didn't really have much to do with me. It wasn't like I was going to live there . . .

I lived here.

As he swiped through a few different houses, I pointed out things that I liked and things I wasn't sure about, but in a disconnected sort of way. In the way you'd give advice to a stranger in Home Depot who asked what you thought of the paint color they'd picked.

Ooohh, that's nice!

I peered at him inquisitively as he looked down at his screen. At thirty-six, his hair had begun to *ever* so slightly salt and pepper. *I hope he doesn't start shaving his beard*, I thought, running my fingers over the coarse white strands.

"What do you think?" he asked.

"About what? Sorry I was zoning out . . ."

"About this place?!" He held up a photo of a glossy front door and started flipping through someone's little suburban dream. Someone's. But certainly not mine.

"Looks super cute. I think smaller places are better, especially since you've always been in a van anyway." I smiled, nudging him playfully.

In that moment, I knew he was asking my opinion because he wanted me to feel like a part of the decision . . . but the idea of that was absolutely paralyzing. I didn't want to be tethered *in any way* to anyone else's plans. Clearly, William didn't want to be tethered to a disheveled trailer that he couldn't even stand all the way up in.

And yet we sat there, side by side, holding hands with matching turquoise rings, planning different lives.

chapter nine

Back to Bend

On the night of October 13, 2018, Bertha barreled through hundreds of miles of pitch-black high desert, going as fast as a vehicle of that age and size *can* go. I'd never been to Bend, Oregon, before, but never in my life had I been happier to see the lights of a city.

The past two hours had been nothing but darkness. Overwhelming darkness, even for someone used to that kind of darkness. No stop signs, no houses, no streetlamps, no gas stations. Nothing but our two headlights.

Neil was at the wheel. I was in the back, lying on the bed, bathed in the warm glow of a string of Christmas lights we'd taped to the van's ceiling when we moved in. An IV bag hung from the wire, swaying methodically like a cuckoo clock. On the other end of it was Dagwood, chest quivering as it rose and fell. He was slowly bleeding to death.

We blinked our matching brown eyes at each other as I begged him through tears to keep his open. I studied his every whisker, every golden hair on his snout, every eyelash, in case this was the last time I'd ever see them.

Neil had run Dagwood over. His fifty-one-pound body bounced beneath the rear tire of our eight-thousand-pound van. It was the tragic accident that changed the trajectory of my life. It was the end of my innocence, my belief that bad things happened to other people. Not us.

It took six hours to get from the remote place we were camping to a hospital that could *actually* help him. The singular small town we'd passed through had one veterinarian, who took one look at him and offered to put him down. His flesh was torn open, his leg broken, his tail ripped from the rest of his spine.

These are images that no amount of time seems to blur. The details are so vivid that I can taste the metallic smell of blood in the back of my throat whenever I think about it.

My therapist has since described this as a hallmark of PTSD.

I don't know if that veterinarian knew for certain that we were the ones who caused these grievous injuries to the thing we loved the most, but she must have sensed the guilt, the absolute despair. She offered up an IV and a heated blanket from a horse stall out back and told us that the nearest hospital was another two hours away. She didn't suspect he'd make it.

But he did. He made it to Bend, Oregon.

For the next thirty-one days, that was where we lived. For the first few nights, we slept in the lobby, or inside of Bertha, who was parked right out front. He was so touch and go that we didn't want to be more than fifty feet away in case they called us in to say goodbye.

He had already had multiple seizures from the blood loss. Despite the fact that he had made it all the way there, he was not expected to survive. He was expected to die, and if not die, then be paralyzed, and if not paralyzed, most certainly incontinent, given the extensive nerve damage from the tail injury and subsequent amputation.

When we finally drove back to Utah, Dagwood still had open wounds, additional surgeries, and months and months of recovery ahead, but he was alive and walking and, to the absolute *shock* of all the surgeons and specialists... pooping on his own.

I still lay in the back beside him, watching his every breath as Bertha crept back into the darkness that had delivered us there an entire month ago. I left harboring that secret that Neil had been the one who hit him. It was information I withheld from the hundreds of thousands of people who had followed along with his remarkable recovery... who had collectively donated all that money. For *my* dog. Who'd been maimed by *my* husband.

Neil was so overcome with guilt and shame in the aftermath that I was afraid it would kill him. I was familiar with how cruel the masses could be, but I knew he wouldn't be able to handle it. So for two years, I kept the secret *for* him, even though he never outright asked me to. I wanted to shield him from it, to hold the door against the battering ram of the internet. But getting Dagwood better felt more urgent than monitoring Neil's every move. Not to mention, physical wounds heal faster than emotional ones.

As I watched the lights of Bend disappear behind us that night, I swore two things: I would never tell anyone, and I would never go back.

"I can't fucking believe I'm going back . . ." I said to my mother four years later, in the summer of 2022. She said something in response, but I couldn't hear it over the dogs barking at the passing cows out in the fields. Fields that had been pitch-black the last time I was on that road.

I tried playing music and then I tried playing true crime podcasts, but I ended up driving in silence, hands shaking, sweating onto Bertha's steering wheel. I would have pulled over to dry heave, but William was behind me in Ruby, followed by his sister, who had flown out to drive my Jeep up in a ragtag two-day caravan from Moab to Bend. So I tried to keep it together.

It was just a two-lane road in central Oregon, but PTSD is a real bitch.

I had finally bit the bullet and found a mechanic in Moab who drove a huge flatbed tow truck up to my property to haul Bertha down to the shop he ran out of his house. She'd been sitting there for almost an entire year at that point, but it was time to get her running.

William had called his friends, who said they'd be happy to fix her up and redo her whole interior setup . . . maybe even install a sink with *running water.* Their shop just happened to be up in Bend.

Despite how offended I was by his attempts to help me with *anything* else, I practically fell at his feet when he offered to help me with

Bertha. *That* was something I knew I'd never accomplish on my own, given that I had spent an entire year refusing even to call a tow truck purely because I didn't want anyone knowing where I lived.

By the time we arrived in Bend, I tried to focus only on Bertha's renovations (in between bouts of turning around to look at Dagwood and make sure he was there and hadn't actually died four years prior).

I couldn't believe this was *finally* happening. I also couldn't believe how much it was estimated to cost for the installation of a high-top, a working sink and stove, heat, air conditioning, and an HGTV-worthy interior renovation. But I always said I'd fix her up, and I intended to follow through.

The shop was more reminiscent of a college dorm party than any of the other dozen or more auto shops I'd had the privilege of spending months in before. The parking lot was full of old custom vans and truck campers and Land Cruisers from the '90s, which everybody knows are the best ones. Almost half of the vehicles had people living inside, so it wasn't uncommon to have a bunch of dirtbags hanging out in the parking lot, leaned up against their rigs, drinking beers from the tap that the shop owners had installed. Every now and again, they'd back a few vans out of the garage to have local bands come and play a rowdy late-night show for fifty-plus friends. When all was said and done, this was the perfect place for Bertha. I trusted all those guys more than some place with a freshly buffed floor in the waiting room and a bunch of guys in uniforms.

William jumped out of the passenger seat and gave bear hugs to all the guys. These were some of his closest friends, and I was meeting them all for the first time, so when I slid Bertha's door open to give the tour, I turned to warn them that there were snakes inside.

They stared at me incredulously as four dogs filed out of the van on either side of me and beelined for the dumpster.

"I'm sorry . . . what???"

"These are my ball pythons, Bean and Mae," I said, flipping back the blankets I'd used to cover their huge tanks for the thirteen-hour journey. "My rat dealer in Moab was watching them for me, but I finally have a consistent place to keep their heat lamps plugged in here now, so I brought them with!"

"Here as in . . . the shop?" one of them asked.

"Rat dealer?!" asked another.

The look on their faces made me want to keep up the gag, but I laughed and said, "No, we got an Airbnb for the month!" Though it's pertinent to mention that I did *not* give such a warning to the owner of said Airbnb. There was a place to list the number of dogs (which I was always truthful about) but there was nowhere on the booking page that asked how many snakes would be coming along.

They were certainly cleaner *and* far quieter than four dogs, so I told myself they probably wouldn't mind.

The shop boys worked diligently on the van, but progress was slow, because progress is *always* slow with Bertha. She is essentially a glued-together pile of recycling, after all.

It became apparent that the entire rebuild was going to take months. Seven months, in fact, was the *minimum* estimate. Unsure of what to do next, we booked the same Airbnb for an additional month, which they accepted, so I'm assuming they hadn't seen us carrying in glass tanks full of pythons under the cover of darkness.

I was living my day-to-day life between the four walls of a house for the first time in years, in a city of a hundred thousand people, no less. (I should note, that is *huge* in my book.)

I left the desert in Bertha, thinking we'd be back down in just a few months' time. I had never rebuilt a van. I had no reference for how long it would take to install lights and outlets and a sink and a stovetop onto the metal frame of a thirty-something-year-old van. Frankly, I had no idea how that was even possible. Bertha had spent the entirety of her life with nothing but a mattress and a bench seat inside and a Coleman camp stove in the back for mac and cheese.

I tried to busy myself with the release of my first book and excitedly updating the internet on Bertha's painfully slow progress. Soon I'd be back on the road, back to where I started. Back to the last time in my life that I felt safe. I didn't register the number of open houses that William was attending, because I still refused to act like his decisions pertained to me at all . . . which, I know full well, was a *bizarre* mindset for someone who just agreed to marry this person.

I knew he loved Bend and had plenty of friends there, but I didn't think he wanted to *live* there. The listings he'd shown me months earlier were all in Salt Lake City, which is only a few hours from Moab. I used to make that drive every single weekend. All of my closest friends still lived there. And I just so happened to be *in* Salt Lake City visiting those friends when he called to tell me he'd bought a house. In Bend.

I've since learned that the housing market operates on urgency. Like one of those cattle auctions where everyone is frantically yelling higher and higher numbers until you forget how much you've even offered. So, it all happened fast.

I sat on my friend's couch, scrolling through the Zillow listing that now read: SOLD in big red letters. It was a 1,500-square-foot single-story, three-bedroom, two-bathroom house. There were skylights in the living room.

And look, a fenced in yard for the dogs! he texted, alongside another photo.

I was happy for him. Congratulations! Go get yourself some champagne!!!

It still hadn't sunk in that he had bought this house with the expectation that we would live there together. Because I already lived somewhere. I already *had* a home, despite the fact that I'd been away from it more in the last few months than I had since I bought it. A house in Bend was not my dream, but clearly, it was his. And I was happy for him. About as happy as I was for a person in Home Depot who found a paint color they liked. In my mind, it had very little, if not nothing, to do with me.

When I drove back up from Salt Lake City in my Jeep, I followed my GPS through a quaint neighborhood, passing a middle school and a park where people were throwing Frisbees for their dogs. Just two blocks from there, we arrived at a little corner house with a wooden fence.

The dogs burst through the front door with far more enthusiasm than I would have expected. So much so that they might as well have run onto an ice rink the way their paws skated and slipped across the wood floors, which were completely bare. The walls were nothing but old nails that once held pictures of someone else's life. While I'd been in Salt Lake, he had transferred a few of our bags and the snakes from the Airbnb to his house.

"You have a *house!*" I shouted excitedly, jumping into his arms with a bottle of champagne in hand. Besides the two forty-gallon glass tanks, there was a single camp chair sitting in the center of what I imagined would become the living room. William ran out to grab another chair from the back of Ruby, which he plopped down beside his own before motioning to it like an usher in a theater.

We sat there drinking champagne, laughing at the fact that we were thirty-two and thirty-seven years old, and neither of us owned a *single* piece of furniture. (I don't count the futon and the bed in my trailer, because they are nailed to the floor.)

It was surreal being there in a completely empty house. It felt like we were on a set. And though I wouldn't have dared admit it, it also felt kind of *exciting*. It was essentially a blank canvas . . . not unlike my property had been.

Over the next few days, we filled the kitchen with a suitable number of random dishes we'd pulled from our respective vans, including a set of teaspoons and measuring cups I'd had since college that had been carefully wrapped inside one of those boxes of clothes I'd been carting around. I hung only one box's worth in the bedroom closet, so it looked like I was visiting . . . not moving in.

William got a mattress, of course, and some other essentials that most people closing in on forty usually have. The Realtor had made sure he knew that the refrigerator would need to be replaced before he signed, so that was one of the first orders of business.

There we stood, side by side, bathed in the fluorescent glow of Home Depot warehouse lighting, staring down two entire aisles of refrigerators. I'm sure I'm making myself sound like some sort of alien, but I had never shopped for, or even thought about, refrigerators or appliances of any kind. How the fuck can there be *that* many options? I mean, why reinvent the wheel? It's a big, cold box for snacks. *Way* bigger than the cooler I used at the trailer because even William couldn't get the fridge in there working. I just taped stuff to it like a bulletin board.

The general consensus seemed to be that refrigerators should be white, black, or silver. Apparently, this goes for all appliances, which I found terribly boring. An employee motioned toward the very end of the aisle where, to my absolute shock and delight, sat an *orange* refrigerator. Nearly a dead ringer for Bertha's paint job, no less. It was made by Samsung, which I thought was a cell phone, but apparently they also make fridges.

And while William did *not* buy the orange fridge, he did agree to let me paint one of the living room walls orange. Which . . . was kind of a big ask. But I told him that I wanted to feel like I was living in Bertha while I waited for her to be done.

"I'm gonna go look at new handles for the cabinets," he said. "You go look at paint, and just grab a bunch of samples if you can't decide!"

I meandered through the aisles, marveling at how every Home Depot looks exactly the same. I damn near grew up in one back in Connecticut given that my dad was a contractor. Despite it being against the rules, he let my brother and me ride on the big, squeaky orange carts designed to carry lumber, and he'd let me take home as many paint swatches as I wanted, despite having absolutely nothing to paint. Then we'd climb back into his work van whose seats were covered in sawdust: a smell that will always make me think of him, even when I don't want to.

An employee startled me out of my daze as I stood in front of a rainbow wall of paint swatches. There were far more orange options than I expected. If I had picked one by then, I might have asked him if he liked it. I might have been comforted by the polite, mundane answer that I'm sure he doled out forty times a day. Perhaps the disinterest in his voice would snap me out of it, remind me of the psychological distance I aimed to keep between me and the wall of someone else's house.

When we got back, William poured himself a whiskey and watched me paint his wall Bertha orange, offering up tips that I pretended not to hear.

The next day, he sat beside me on the new couch, scrolling through Amazon for a dog door that would work for the sliding glass door out to the yard. When it arrived, he was prepared to teach them how to use it. But before he could so much as pack up his tools, they burst through it one by one into the yard, sprinting toward one particular scrub jay that had been taunting them since we showed up.

I watched each one of them obsessively, making sure they weren't depressed or confused, but they had been to so many Airbnbs and friends' houses and hotels and motels and vans and trailers and tents over the years that *home* to them had already become wherever I was. And vice versa.

It didn't take very long at all for each of them to settle on their own spots throughout the house. Dagwood loved to lie on the floor in the office under William's desk, while Bucket took over the entire second bedroom the moment a mattress appeared in there.

Birdie was wherever I was at all times, so not much had changed there. And Banjo spent most of his time burrowing under the old wooden deck and then littering the yard with the remnants of whatever rodents he'd killed. (It was very apparent which of them had only *ever* grown up completely wild.)

William built two custom, weight-bearing shelves for Bean's and Mae's cages in the closet of the third bedroom, which he decided would be his office. He removed the door entirely, then installed a little ventilation system and a timer that would automatically adjust their heating lamps.

From the day we met, he knew the best way to me was through my animals.

One afternoon, as I stood in line at Barnes & Noble, a cookbook caught my eye. I don't remember why, exactly. I just remember being excited to buy a cookbook and bring it back to the kitchen that I had just painted green. (Asking to paint the kitchen green after you've already painted the living room orange is much easier.)

On the way back, I stopped at Target and picked out all kinds of pots and pans and an entire rack of spices that I'd always wanted but never had a place for and, really, no reason to use. I found some pretty stemmed glassware and a few dish towels to hang from the oven.

These ones had green and yellow flowers on them, unlike the one in my trailer that had a picture of a woman wrestling an alligator beneath the words DO ONE THING EVERY DAY THAT SCARES YOUR FAMILY.

I chose a few throw blankets for the couches and decorative pillows and dozens of candles and one of those special little cups for toothbrushes. Then I wheeled my cart over to the checkout and stood in line with everybody else.

Because "everybody else" is who it felt like I was becoming.

When I'd moved into Bertha all those years ago, it required me to do a broad, sweeping rejection of everything I saw as a "normal life." I had to *really* commit to the whole vagabond, vanlife, dirtbag thing if I planned to fully denounce the world I'd fled from. I was a wanderer, a free spirit, a nomad. That's what I was known for. That's what I built my entire life *and* career around.

When you spend almost a decade demonstrating (and then endlessly *defending*) the way you've chosen to live, it's impossible to separate it from your identity.

To have people find out that I was now spending months on end in a cute little house in a quaint suburban neighborhood with a front seat full of Target bags and a fiancé who wanted to "take care of me"? I felt like a vegan who'd been caught eating a cheeseburger.

See! You're not who you say you are!

. . .

homesick nomad

I liked it better when you were in your trailer in the desert! some folks would whine on Instagram, as if my life was a Netflix show and this new season wasn't living up to their expectations.

How funny would it be if she announces that she's pregnant next! another posted on the Reddit, which ignited a firestorm of cliché responses from a bunch of other participants about how I was probably going to start "wearing aprons and making sourdough bread."

(To be fair, I *had* bought myself an apron for William's kitchen, but it said THE FOOD HAS WEED IN IT across the chest. And regardless of my living situation, I can't imagine I'll ever have the patience to make sourdough.)

It felt like those people had been waiting with bated breath for me to "give up" and go back to having more standardized life dreams. Dreams that didn't make them compulsively analyze and compare their own. *You've had your fun playing dress-up in the desert, now it's time to settle down like a well-behaved thirtysomething.*

I loved William, and I was actually starting to love that orange wall and the green kitchen cabinets, and even some of those stupid throw pillows. But it still all felt so . . . sterile to me. As if I had ended up in the suburbs doing loads of laundry all the time and rotting at stoplights with all the people I said I would never be like.

Day after day, I waited for news of Bertha, not only because I wanted her back, but because I wanted to have something to post that would prove to everyone that I was still who I said I was. When

I'd driven her up to Bend, I'd felt like I was getting *closer* to all my goals. Now, I felt farther away from any of them than I ever had. But how could I sit there and tell this man I loved that his dream felt like it was replacing mine entirely? How could I *love* being called "baby," while also feeling like *any* gesture of caretaking meant I was being treated like one?

When I lay in bed each night, I thought of those desert horizons and my trailer and the way the sheer white curtains caught even the slightest breeze. I missed how the sunrise was always cotton candy pink. And with the exception of those occasional storms, the sunsets were always deep, lighting up the tippy tops of the sandstone so it glowed like the guiding beacon of a lighthouse.

Then William would scooch in behind me, pulling me closer into the shape of him, and I would remember why I was there. I would remember that no matter how much I fought against myself, the feelings I had for him weren't going away.

My solace was taking the dogs out every day to a network of totally unimpressive dirt roads where folks would go for target practice. I knew this, because the area was riddled with Bud Light cans, shotgun shells, and couches pumped full of bullet holes.

There was nothing particularly beautiful about it, but it reminded me of being home because there was scarcely anyone there. I'd managed to find us a safe corner of a crowded place. Another place to hide. I could think much more clearly as soon as my tires touched that dirt.

One morning, I decided to switch things up and drive us high up into the Cascade Mountains where the Douglas firs and western hemlocks nearly block out the sky. I got lost out there wandering beneath them. And not in a whimsical, Henry David Thoreau kind of way, like, *actually* lost in the woods.

I tried to remember which way I'd come from, which forest service road I'd chosen at one of the many intersections of nondescript forest roads. There was nothing but trees in every direction. It all looked exactly the same to me. In the desert, you can always look out at the expansive horizon and pinpoint where you came from... where you need to get back to. There's so much sky to light up, so many stars to follow like the old cowboys did. The days feel longer, the passing of time less urgent.

In the thick of the forest, I attempted to use what I could see of the sun as a compass and track my own footprints like a hunter stalking prey. The dogs ran every which way at all times so their footprints weren't reliable at all.

When I finally caught sight of my Jeep parked beneath one of twelve billion trees, Dagwood was standing in front of it proudly, as if to say, *My nose works better out here than your eyes.*

William noticed pretty early on that I refused to call it "our house," and especially not "*my* house." Even in chatting with his friends, I'd say, "Y'all should come over to William's house this weekend!"

In my mind *and* on paper . . . it really wasn't my house. And I sure as hell wouldn't want William calling my place in Utah "*his* property." I did that on my own, just like he had bought that house on his own. Perhaps I'm just sensitive to giving credit where I believe credit is due because accomplishing anything like that on your own is a big fucking deal. But more likely, I was trying so hard not to become attached to something that didn't belong to me in any way . . . something that was totally out of my control.

I was too scared to admit to anyone that there were things I had started to really like about being in that house. Picking movies to watch each night and ordering Indian takeout from "our favorite place" and taking showers more frequently than I had in years, though I still get bored being in there for more than five minutes.

I was so resistant to liking it that I tried to convince myself I hated it instead. I called my mother after only a few months and told her, quite dramatically, that this house was "killing my spirit."

Bertha was light-years away from being done, so I packed my Jeep up instead and took off back to Utah. I cried the moment the red rocks of Moab appeared over my steering wheel thirteen hours later. I cried even harder when I pulled up my driveway to find my trailer roasting in the sun, untouched as if we'd only been at My Beach for the day.

The dogs ran wildly around the yard, darted in and out of the trailer, and proceeded to massacre a bunch of lizards who'd grown accustomed to having unfettered access to every sunny rock while we were gone. They'd have to go back to being stealthy, but lizards are good at that.

That very afternoon, I texted William a photo of my legs splayed out on my lounge chair, soaking in my sixth straight hour of sun.

So happy you're there, baby, he replied. I have a surprise for you when you get back. (William always says he has a surprise and then goes on to tell you immediately what that surprise is, which I very much appreciated as a deeply impatient person and as someone who had yet to decide *when* exactly I was coming back.)

The next text he sent was a picture of the backyard.

When he bought the place, the fenced-in area only took up about half the allotted yard space. In my absence, he had hired someone to expand the fence in every single direction, flush up to the final inch, just shy of a town zoning violation.

Lord knows how much he paid for it. I'd been floored at how much seemingly standard house things cost. But he had made sure that Bucket, Dagwood, Birdie, and Banjo had *every last inch* of space to run.

I sat there, shocked. "He made you an even bigger yard, Birdie," I said, since she had immediately jumped on my lap the moment tears started forming in the corners of my eyes.

The next photo he sent was of a lounge chair out in the grass. It was almost identical to the one at my property . . . the one I was sitting on at that very moment.

So you can sit in the sun as much as you like, he wrote.

chapter ten

What's Yours Is Yours

William knew that if he tried to rope me, I'd run. His gestures often felt like someone leaving food out for a feral dumpster cat, hoping one day they'll feel safe enough to come inside.

For a long time, our relationship was a bit of a standoff. Neither of us would dare infringe on each other's freedoms, so there was never any talk of *I want you to be in Bend more* or *It would mean a lot to me if you'd spend more time with me in Moab*.

People's eyebrows rose clear up to their hairline when I'd say, "My fiancé and I live in different states." I absolutely refused to say I lived in Oregon. I also refused to change my driver's license *or* my plates *or* my mailing address, which was why I missed several important letters from the IRS that were sitting in my post office box in Moab for months.

. . .

homesick nomad

William flew to Alaska for a two-week photoshoot, leaving me alone at the house for the first time. (With Bucket, Dagwood, Birdie, Banjo, Bean, and Mae, of course.)

After I dropped him at the airport, I returned to the house where I proceeded to wander around like a grown-up version of Macaulay Culkin in *Home Alone*, sitting on the kitchen counter, smoking a joint, looking around at how clean everything was. He kept everything so *clean*.

Getting out of bed in the morning, my feet would hit the smooth wooden floors. He had one of those robots that made its way around the house each day, smashing into walls and scaring the bejesus out of the dogs. Except for Dagwood, who was so unbothered he would actually lie there and let it repeatedly ram into his sleeping back. Occasionally he'd lift his head and look back at it, annoyed.

The floor of my trailer had so much dirt on it each morning that it felt more like stepping out of bed onto my gravel driveway.

When I got up to use the bathroom at night, I'd instinctually look up, only to find myself boxed in by a plain white ceiling. Not a star in sight. One evening, I went out into the backyard and peed in the grass just for fun. Banjo looked down at me from atop the picnic table where he slept almost every night (by choice, of course).

Regardless of whether either of us had service or not, we never felt the need to speak on the phone all the time. We didn't always say good night, and we didn't always say good morning. We'd just chat intermittently throughout the day when little things reminded us of each other, like '90s country love songs he wished he'd written as letters to me, or pictures of each and every animal I met in my travels. To me, it felt more genuine than some forced check-in, as if reporting to a parent.

What did feel quite "parental" was the fact that he had to text me to remind me which days were recycling and garbage days, which I obviously forgot immediately, but I didn't want to admit that I had, so I drove the garbage around town until I spotted an unsupervised dumpster. That was how I threw out my garbage every day in Moab, so it was no sweat off my back.

When William got back from that trip, we had our first real argument. I would make something to eat, drop my dishes into the sink, and walk away. I'd always do them by the end of the day . . . or the next . . . but it drove William nuts and he never failed to point it out to me.

"Here I am in some man's house, being made to do the dishes!!" I lamented to my mother on the phone *yet again*. Mind you, they were *my* fucking dishes! But I had such a violent, knee-jerk reaction to anything and everything that made me feel like I'd become "a housewife" doing chores in a man's kitchen made me a failure to wild women everywhere.

My mother, meanwhile, loved those kinds of responsibilities. She wasn't a "housewife" per se, as she still worked five days a week, but one look at the house she lived in with her boyfriend, and you'd never know it.

She wiped every surface immediately after breathing on it, and the carpets and rugs always had fresh vacuum lines in them. She was an amazing interior decorator, always opting for a vintage, shabby chic look, and her garden out front was award-winning.

One summer when I drove across the country to see all my old friends and their very new babies, my mom and her boyfriend were kind enough to let me stay with them for a whole month with all four of my dogs.

My childhood dog, Lola, who had lived to be nearly nineteen years old, was the only animal that had ever lived in that house, and she was a Chihuahua who weighed four pounds at most.

I was in Utah when she died. Late one night, Mom called from the emergency vet and put me on speakerphone next to her so we could both talk to her right up until the very end. My mother said it was harder than her divorce.

There hadn't been any dogs in that house since, so allowing my wolf pack to stampede through their front door and onto their almost exclusively white furniture was quite the gesture of goodwill.

Not to mention, Bertha sat outside dripping oil onto the driveway, which she did absolutely all the time. One morning I walked out to find that my mother had duct-taped gigantic pieces of cardboard onto the pavement beneath the van to... "protect the asphalt."

"I wouldn't want him to have to redo his driveway," she said in a hushed voice, as if he might be listening, despite the fact that he was out playing golf.

Interestingly enough, she had moved into that house over a *decade* ago by then... but still, it was *his* driveway. *His* house. Runs in the family, I suppose.

Perhaps because "the family" we once had scattered like bomb debris after my parents' divorce. Even my grandparents, aunts, uncles, and cousins on my dad's side retired from any role they had played in my childhood. Despite the fact that he is alive and well and living in Florida, the last time I saw or spoke to my paternal grandfather, I was eleven years old. Based on the track record of the men in my family, it's no wonder all the women ended up so strong whether they wanted to or not.

My brother and I, though close in age, had never been close in any other way. It's often hard to believe we shared the same womb. I was deeply emotional about it all, but when I tried to talk to him about any of it, he was steely, annoyed even. He suggested that I get over it. "Just fucking move on already," he'd say, as if being abandoned by your father is as easy to get over as a grade-school breakup.

Granted, he was just a teenager at the time. We both were. But he was the only person in the whole world who knew *exactly* what I was going through. He lost the same father, the same family, the same childhood home, the same idea of what the future might look like. Whatever he felt, if he felt anything at all, was locked away. Sometimes I think it still is.

Our childhood was beautiful, and then it was gone. I was fifteen years old when we packed up and drove away. I was fifteen years old the last time I'd ever confidently called something *my house*. That was the last time it ever felt like the truth.

chapter eleven

The Science of Packing

Once I realized that doing the dishes and vacuuming up whatever that stupid little robot missed wasn't spousal abuse, I made a more conscious effort around the house.

I had always been pretty disorganized, but that wasn't some deeply important personality trait worth protecting. Having things in order and relatively clean *was* important to William. (I say "relatively," because allowing four dogs into your house comes with the obvious understanding that you're never going to be able to eat off the floor.)

I decided that I could still be a freewheeling, half-naked wild woman while wiping the countertops, because it was just something nice to do for the person I loved. What I started to realize was that this was the kind of relationship I'd quietly needed all along.

As antifeminist as it may sound to some, I needed a man who could keep me accountable. Someone who would challenge me, call me out, not let me bulldoze my way through everything. I needed someone a bit more unyielding, more hardened, so, perhaps for the first time in my life, I could feel safe enough to soften.

I tried bringing my new cleaning routines to my trailer, where they lasted approximately forty-eight hours. Rome wasn't built in a day, you know? The only routine that stuck no matter where I was, was packing.

For years on end, there had scarcely been a few weeks in which I wasn't packing *some* bag to go *some*where.

Besides my regular thirteen-hour drive back and forth from Moab to Bend, I was hosting international group travel trips that took me all over the world. If William couldn't watch the dogs, I was lucky enough to have friends from Oregon down to Utah who would.

Oftentimes, when I left William's house, I was packing for three different trips in three different climates. I up and left so often that I wouldn't even bother to unpack suitcases. In fact, I would only unpack them when it was time to repack them, which I would usually do forty-five minutes before I had to leave for the airport.

Half of my outdoor gear was in William's garage in Bend, and the other half was scattered across my property, shoved into a trailer drawer, or tossed between the now *two* storage units I had in Moab.

My dogs, my Rollerblades, and my paddleboard were usually the only things I consistently carted with me wherever I was going. (When I traveled via car, not plane, obviously.)

I tried to line up my package deliveries depending on which state I was going to be in, but that was futile, as I'd often jump up out of bed as if from a fever dream and declare that I *had* to go to

Utah the very next day. My feet would get itchy quite suddenly and quite often.

I was away from the house in Bend often enough to forget where light switches were, which cabinet held the cutting board... I couldn't find a damn thing in that town without GPS. One solution to my back-and-forthness came in the form of having two of everything. Two pharmacies, two hairdressers, two different mailing addresses, two different veterinarians...

"Oh shit, I'm supposed to be at the dentist in Bend tomorrow," I'd mutter aloud to the dogs as we tumbled down some red dirt road in Moab. My cancellation fees were easily in the four-digit range.

My life was—in almost every sense of the word—*all* over the place. Although it had technically been all over the place since my mid-twenties, which might explain why I still think of myself as being that age.

William scarcely knew where he was going to be either. Trying to get plans on both of our calendars for anything more than a month in advance was pointless. We'd sit down side by side, or have a FaceTime from two faraway places. We'd call it "doing schedules," which was basically us trying to figure out when we might see each other again.

His schedule was far more "legitimate" than mine, given that much of his travel was for work, whereas much of my travel was for running off with the dogs to be naked in the desert somewhere.

His work took him all over the country, all over the world even. Whenever he wasn't at the house, I didn't see a reason for me to be.

Over the first two years of our relationship, we saw each other for less than half of each.

When we *were* in Bend together, William seemed content to kick his boots up and just watch me flitter in circles all around the house, talking a million miles a minute, packing up and leaving every other week, wandering the house half naked with a python around my neck and Fleetwood Mac blasting from the record player. He had surprised me with the *Rumours* album one afternoon for no reason in particular.

Each time I went back up to Oregon, I'd add more *me* to the house. Eventually, there were suncatchers in every window that sent little rainbow orbs dancing across the room, bouncing off the dusty-rose-colored velvet couch.

I bought it because it was significantly bigger than the first one he picked, and it was very important to me that all *six* of us had our own place to sit. I made sure to get one without springs so the snakes couldn't get stuck when they'd slither off my shoulders to explore in the cushions while we watched TV.

I'm not sure where I got the idea, but I spent one evening installing a huge (fake) crystal chandelier in my closet (which was a whopping three feet by four feet and also painted orange). I couldn't even reach up to grab any of my cowboy boots off the shelf without knocking into it, casting a dizzying light over my clothes. By then, I was feeling brave enough to hang *three* boxes' worth.

. . .

Over time, *sterile* became the last word anyone would use to describe that house. In some ways, it was reminiscent of my property in Moab.

The front yard wasn't pristinely landscaped; in fact, you couldn't even really see it because it was hidden beneath Ruby and Bertha (whose build was finally finished, but now she needed an entire new wiring harness, which would take God knows how long). She was too big for the driveway, so I parked her directly on the front lawn. I was just happy to be able to look at her again every day, even if she still had a long way to go to be road ready.

There was my Jeep, of course, as well as an old Land Cruiser that William had bought. In the side yard, there was a wooden sailboat that he'd gotten for a whopping five hundred bucks on Facebook Marketplace. It even came with a trailer that was backed up on the side of the house in front of *another* Jeep that had been rusting on his family farm in Illinois since the 1950s. He planned to restore it one day, and I believed that he would. William really is the type to follow through on a project like that, whereas some folks might spend years letting the grass grow up around it. (By "some folks," I mean me.)

As for the backyard, it was littered with dog toys and an entire outdoor furniture set that I had taken to calling "my environment," since I spent almost all of my time out there in the warmer months, roasting in the sun like I did no matter where I was. William affectionately referred to me as a lizard in my backyard aquarium.

There was also a firepit, a couple of grills, and a bright pink, inflatable baby pool that Bucket and I would sit in together.

One afternoon, I shot up from the couch and announced that I was going to build a tiki bar in the yard. I suspect he thought I was going to go to some party store and buy a few fake flower leis and plastic cups and a grass skirt to tape around the front of the picnic table.

Instead, I spent the next three days straight building an entire bar from scratch. This shocked even me, as I had never so much as nailed a birdhouse together on my own. I'd built that godforsaken shed down at my place, but it was plastic and came with a seven-hundred-page Ikea-esque instruction manual. This I would be constructing entirely with my own two hands (and plenty of tools William lent me).

I drove back and forth from Home Depot multiple times a day, trying to ignore that sentimental sawdust smell. I'd return to the house each time with massive piles of wood sticking out of the rear hatch window of the Jeep. Two-by-fours and four-by-fours and six-by-fours and whatever size comes after that.

I did borrow William's Land Cruiser the day that I went to pick up 1,800 pounds of sand in the form of about forty bags. The rear suspension held on for dear life as I slowly rolled out of the parking lot.

Besides borrowing his car and asking him to show me how to use a few of the saws I wasn't familiar with, I wouldn't allow him to help. He didn't insist, let alone ask. He knew better by then. He did, however, watch me nervously through a window while I got comfortable with the angle saw. I caught a glimpse of him through the glass and yelled, "Go away! It's my legal right to cut off my own finger!"

He'd come out to check my progress or bring me lunch or just stare incredulously at what was starting to look like a *real* tiki bar. I'd even ordered two huge rolls of dried thatched roofing.

When it was completed, I bought a few neon signs: one, a flamingo; the other, an arrow that said LIVE NUDES. I'd sometimes hang that one on the front door of the house when William went out to do an errand so he'd be greeted by it on his way back in.

He wasn't always enthused by that one, but I had to remind him that no one could even see the front door anyway because it was hidden behind a car show's worth of vehicles. Bertha was quite literally as tall as the house. And who fucking cares anyway?!

The best part about the tiki bar—and the whole backyard in general—was that the houses surrounding it were all single-story, meaning no one could see *into* the yard, meaning I could lie topless on the chaise lounge just like I did at home.

Between the car show on the lawn, the orange wall, the chandelier in the closet, the constant nudity, and now this (shockingly impressive!) tiki bar I had built from scratch ... I started to feel like I hadn't lost myself as much as I'd once feared.

In the winter of 2022, we decided not to go to Baja like we had the year before. We decided ... well, *I* decided ... to stay in Bend for three months straight. That would be the longest stint I'd ever pulled.

I convinced myself that it was the responsible thing to do, given an upcoming deadline for my second book, but there was also a part of me that wanted to know what it would be like to wake up morning after morning after morning in the same place with a warm fire and a hot shower.

For the first month, I leaned in. I wrapped myself in cozy sweaters and made cheesecakes in my weed apron and walked the dogs out in the woods with much more confidence now because I could retrace my footsteps in the snow.

By the second month, I felt like a vegetable. A potato, to be exact. It did not help that I've always suffered terribly from seasonal depression, but the darkness combined with the sameness was driving me to the brink.

One weekend, when William was away on another shoot, it occurred to me that I should probably order a fully operational disco ball to hang from the living room ceiling. Due to being in a city the size of Bend, I was able to overnight it, which was quite a treat, since getting mail to Moab is a three-day minimum *at best*.

It was simple enough to install and came with a little remote control. I blew out all the candles, because I still preferred to live like that when William was out of town. He was keener on controlling the mood lighting in the house via an app on his phone. (This actually came in handy given how often I'd forget which switches went to which lights.)

With a click of the remote, the room filled with spinning reds and yellows and greens and blues. It was big enough and bright enough to send huge orbs floating across the refrigerator clear on the other side of the room. I was suddenly glad William had decided on a stainless steel one, because it basically acted as a reflector, making everything look even more colorful.

The dogs watched me from their designated couch cushions as I spun around the room, blasting music from the surround sound speakers that William had installed, though he scarcely cranked the volume to its full potential.

I sprinted to my closet, flipping through the hangers until I came upon the full-body sequin jumpsuit I'd worn on my birthday in New Orleans. It shimmered in the light of the chandelier as I slipped into it.

Snow fell softly around the house as I jumped up onto the coffee table, startling Banjo who lay sleeping beneath it, as I shimmied and sang along (poorly) to Donna Summer.

And it was only then that I remembered something I'd forgotten. In fact, I jumped down from the coffee table and rushed to my phone to send a text.

Mom, do you remember all those nights at Christine's?

Across the street and two doors down from my childhood house was where Christine lived with her two boys. They were younger than me, but we could all still be considered grade-schoolers.

Christine was divorced, worked as a chef, and made my mom laugh all the time. She was brash and unapologetic and completely magnetic. One Wednesday night, she invited us over. I know for certain it was a Wednesday, because it was always a Wednesday thereafter.

My mom and I walked across the street, hand in hand, with another one of our neighbors, Gail, and her daughter Ava.

Christine swung open the bright red door and ushered us inside. As mentioned, my mother's style was antique and delicate, and there was a doily on every table surface, and *everything* was white. Even the wooden tables and chairs she'd find at the antique store would get spray-painted white in the driveway before they crossed the threshold.

Everything at my house was *just so*, the same way it was in all of my other friends' houses, as if there might be an inspection at any moment, as if there was one Connecticut-wide interior decorator who went around doling out the same sensible-colored furniture and placing seashells on every windowsill in the state.

But when Christine opened the door—wine in hand—she invited us into a house unlike any I'd ever seen. (At least not in real life.)

The living room was purple with black velvet couches and white fuzzy pillows. Her bedroom was bright pink with an elaborate light fixture. There were artful statues of women adorning most of the tabletops and brightly colored paintings on nearly every wall.

It was *worlds* different than the house I grew up in just two hundred feet away. I'd been so quick to assume that all the houses I hadn't been in were exactly the same as the ones I had.

Christine came back into the purple living room holding a Rubbermaid box of feather boas and fun glasses and a disco ball you could plug in on the floor.

My mother might have been a poised and polished woman, but she danced freely and without hesitation, no matter where we were. To this day, she still pulls me onto the dance floor the moment any music starts playing, just like she has since I was a little girl.

Christine and Gail and my mom would go crazy when Donna

Summer's "Bad Girls" came on. Her two sons, Ava, and I used the coffee table as a stage while they danced around us in circles. They would always sing the "toot toot!" part into their pretend microphones, then hold them up to us to sing back, "Beep beep!"

It was nothing but a little lights and music and colorful paint on the walls and a woman who didn't rightly care if her house looked like anyone else's . . . but it was a memory from my childhood that I'd long forgotten, buried beneath everything else that followed.

The recollections of my childhood in Connecticut are often tainted. Perhaps because of that perceived mandatory rejection of it all. Perhaps because of that need to feel "different" than everybody else.

And so my mind, in all its stubborn glory, took creative control of the full picture of my upbringing. It summarized it, SparkNoted it, abbreviated it. I lumped everyone together as *they* because I was convinced that was the only way to be *me*.

It wasn't until twenty years later, when I hung my own disco ball from the ceiling in front of an orange wall, that I realized . . . *where* you are doesn't matter as much once you know *who* you are.

chapter twelve

You'll Change Your Mind

"When the time comes to have a baby, you'll have some challenges."

It's startling how quickly you can conjure up a whole life to flash before your eyes despite having never lived it . . . having barely even thought about it.

Besides coming up with a list of Grateful Dead–related baby names in high school, my only *real* thoughts of pregnancy and motherhood thus far had been how to avoid it. I was only nineteen years old, after all.

The doctor stood over my loose-limbed, sprawled-out body on the hospital bed. They'd given me intravenous morphine for the pain, and thank God they did because it is, to date, the most physical pain I've ever been in.

"They're no joke, these ovarian cysts," the doctor said, patting my shoulder like a coach. "Folks compare them to labor pains!" Which was sort of ironic given the news he'd just delivered. "Especially ones like this," he said, holding up my ultrasound. He shook his head side to side, clicking his tongue as if he was disappointed by my internal organs.

It was estimated that the cyst on my ovary was about the size of a grapefruit when it ruptured. It was also hemorrhagic, so it filled my body with blood and fluid, leaving my stomach bizarrely distended and firm, almost as if I *was* pregnant.

The diagnosis was polycystic ovarian syndrome, a hormonal disorder that prevents ovulation, along with a few other lovely side effects like the one I had just experienced.

The doctor assured me it was manageable.

"Hormonal birth control should actually prevent the cysts from getting large enough to rupture." He spoke about it as if it were no problem at all until he dropped the whole baby thing. His tone shifted drastically, his voice somber, as if he were delivering news of a death.

After I was discharged, I sat out in the parking lot, staring over my steering wheel toward the freeway. It was winter and the setting sun was streaming through the windshield onto the faded black seats, making everything feel warm. I closed my eyes.

A doctor had just told me that I might not be able to have children. My mind raced, but kept landing back on one nagging thought. *Am I supposed to be . . . sadder than I am right now?*

I mean, sure, I was rattled in the sense that I'd just been given a new medical diagnosis, but I was more preoccupied by what I couldn't bring myself to feel. For a good twenty minutes, I sat there trying to catch just one racing thought for long enough to make sense of it.

Am I defective? Isn't this what women live for? Don't they say this is the ultimate goal, the highest possible purpose? Aren't people without children so pitied, so tiptoed around as if not to break their surely shattered spirits?

Now, it's important to note that no doctor had indicated that I could *never* get pregnant. But it was still the first time that motherhood was presented to me as a possibility, as opposed to a certainty.

When I left that day, it felt like I'd been given a doctor's note allowing me to sit out of gym class permanently. I was off the hook.

By the time I got married at the tender young age of twenty-four, I was absolutely certain that I would never have children of my own. It's such a weighted sentence, even writing it over a decade later still feels like some sort of obituary for other people's expectations.

Mostly because during all those years I was inevitably met with one of the same old responses from a Rolodex of clichés.

You'll change your mind was the most common one folks seemed to land on. Since I was in my early twenties, I'm sure it seemed like a no-brainer.

Now, remember, I *was* working in Utah County, just south of Salt Lake, which was—and still is—in the top five counties in the entire country when it comes to birthrates.

Because giving birth was all the rage around there, I almost felt the need to preface my responses with an apology of sorts. "I'm sure it's wonderful, but . . ." or "Oh I *love* kids, I just . . ."

I really *do* love kids, by the way (well . . . some kids), but loving children and not wanting children of your own seems to be something folks struggle to compute.

Eventually I just started to lie.

I'd say, "Oh, we'll see . . ." with a polite smile. Frankly, I would have started telling people I'd just taken a positive pregnancy test that very morning if I thought it would get them off my back.

I was tired of being told that if I *didn't* change my mind, I would never know true love and would surely die alone after living a life completely void of purpose.

If I was in a particular mood, I'd respond with something a little more startling.

"When are you and your husband going to have a baby?"

"Ohhh, I actually have a medical issue that makes getting pregnant *very* difficult," I'd reply with an exaggerated frown.

It wasn't a lie, after all, and sometimes it's important to make people realize how intimate a question they've just asked a total stranger.

My in-laws, however, had no reservations about intimate questions. Neil had left me the task of breaking the news that we weren't having children, the same way I'd broken the news that we weren't getting married in a church. It had always been up to *me* to defend *our* decisions. I suppose that's just another reason I ended up being so damn good at it.

His parents were distraught. I was, in essence, the daughter-in-law of their nightmares. A tattooed atheist who didn't want children and preferred, instead, to live in a very, very old van with dogs she treated as such.

Before we even got married, Neil's older brother had let the whole family know that I wasn't "wife material."

Regardless, their disappointment emboldened me. Their disdain for my choice made me feel like it was the right one. Because I've never felt like I was cut out for doing what everybody else was doing, simply because everybody else was doing it. All I know is that I've always had a deep, nagging *knowing* about myself. An internal compass set for God knows where, but set nonetheless.

Fortunately, my own mother never really batted an eye. She may have said "You'll change your mind" at some point before I got married, but when she realized that I wasn't going to, she just shrugged and said, "Well, you always did prefer stuffed animals to baby dolls..."

The first time I posted anything on Instagram about my decision to not have children, I was a bit hesitant. At the time I had maybe seventy thousand followers, so it was a little different than announcing it to Neil's family at the dinner table.

I was shocked, however, to find that complete strangers seemed just as disappointed as the people who *were* at that dinner table.

A comment—one of *many*—on that first post said, Imagine if your mom felt the same way! You wouldn't even be here to write this!

Now, of course, it's nice that my mother had me, but it's not like I would have known the difference if she hadn't. And her support of me not wanting kids of my own never once made me feel like she hadn't wanted me. If anything, it made me feel *more* wanted. My mother brought me into this world to see who I would become... to watch me bloom into some raggedy wildflower in a desert field somewhere, because she knew that keeping me in her pristine, award-winning garden just wouldn't have been fair to me.

Her support of my decision made me feel like an individual, not just another woman in a long line of women who are expected to mindlessly do what women have always done.

That remark was pretty uneventful compared to the others. After all, most social media comment sections tend to provide a full rectal temperature of society's views on any given topic.

My personal favorites were all the folks just desperate to know who was going to take care of me when I was too old to care for myself. People say this with a sense of profound certainty that makes me wonder if they've ever even driven *past* a nursing home, let alone been inside of one.

Another classic was the concern that I would have "no one to carry on my family legacy." Which, to me, has always sounded like someone who is either cosplaying some *Game of Thrones* character, or just someone who takes themselves *way* too seriously.

The most common consensus, however, was that women without children owed people an explanation.

What's wrong with children?!

Why wouldn't you want to have children?!

How sad!! My children are my greatest joy!!!!

Mind you, I can't recall the last time I asked anyone why they *have* children. Imagine looking at photos of someone's newborn baby and saying, "What if you change your mind?" You'd be societally cast out.

To be perfectly honest, I wish that *was* normal. I wish we asked young people *why* they want to have children, instead of *when* they want to have children.

But becoming a mother is looked at as an eventuality, so girls don't ask an awful lot about it. We just dress up our dollies and our teddy bears and all the grown-ups pat the tops of our heads and say, "What a good mommy you're going to be!" You're *going* to be.

Even the doctor all those years ago had said "when" the time comes.

It's a far-off, yet somehow inescapable notion that girls grow up with, but the gravity of the decision—or the concept of it being a *decision* at all—seems to be lost entirely.

In the United States, the average woman gives birth to her first child at the age of twenty-seven. When *I* was twenty-seven, I had just quit my well-paying corporate job to move into a van. By thirty-four, I'd driven across the United States six times. I'd been to Canada, Perú, Argentina, Ecuador, Cambodia, Malaysia, Laos. I hopped a plane to Nicaragua one winter just to go learn how to surf. (For the record, I wasn't very good.)

I'd swum with humpback whales in Tahiti; ridden camels in Wadi Rum, Jordan; floated in a hot-air balloon as the sun rose over Cappadocia, Turkey. I'd hugged an elephant's trunk in South Africa, slept on the dunes of the Sahara in Morocco, backpacked through New

Zealand, walked beside Komodo dragons as the sun set on an island in Indonesia. I had dinner by myself in Dubai at the top of the tallest building in the world because I'd gotten stuck there unintentionally when my visa to get into India was rejected. (Paperwork issue.)

I'd been canyoneering and rock climbing and snowboarding and mountain biking and white-water rafting and skydiving and BASE jumping and bungee jumping and every other way you can think of to huck yourself into a freefall. I had spent four winters in a row on the beach in Mexico with my dogs... just because I could.

I share this long, run-on, gloating paragraph for one reason only: If I'd had a *child* at twenty-seven instead of a Ford E-350, I wouldn't have been able to do all of that. Surely not by thirty-five. And I think that's worth being pretty damn proud of. And it's most certainly worth being honest about, despite the fact that this sentiment sends some folks into a tizzy too.

"People with kids can do all of this!!!"

(Interestingly, this is often said by the *very* same people who see you off riding camels and jumping out of airplanes and living in your car and say, "Enjoy it while you can!! You won't be able to do this when you have kids!" Talk about mixed messaging...)

By my mid-thirties, I'd gone from being the woman who said she wasn't having kids, to the woman who didn't have kids. Plenty of my friends back east had become moms by then, but it didn't *really* hit me until three of my closest friends in Utah announced that they were pregnant, each with a little girl, all within a few months of each other.

When the first one announced, I was thrilled. When the second one announced, I was ecstatic. When the third announcement came, I was overjoyed and *overcome* with anxiety.

I'd known for years that this was going to happen, but when it was actually happening, it knocked me off my feet. One, because in my Peter Pan brain, I still believed we were too young to have babies, and two, because I could never have anticipated feeling so incredibly... lonely.

It's one thing to say you'll end up on a different path someday, but it's something else entirely to look down and realize that you're really on it. Because the question of motherhood has two standard answers and one fork in the road. To be a mother or to be *not* a mother. You either are or you aren't.

To *be* a mother is to enter into a worldwide collective of relatabilities. There is a profound and universal meaning that comes along with that title. There are Instagrams and TikToks dedicated to parenting advice, support groups for mothers, (well-deserved) dedicated holidays, mommy-and-me meetups...

The act of simply *having* a child is enough common ground for women to form entire relationships over. There is solace in experiencing the same milestones, even if there are hundreds of different ways to go about them.

To *not* be a mother feels less like a path and more like splitting off into the woods like a disjointed militia with no clear destination. There's no automatic common ground, no inherent sameness. The one thing we all have in common is most likely the number of times we've been made to defend our decisions.

There are seldom "support groups" for women who have *chosen* not to be mothers. If there are, they're usually infiltrated by folks who believe that the participants are just secretly miserable about their choice to be child-free. As if acknowledging that a choice can feel lonely at times means that you regret it entirely. (Though, on behalf of children everywhere, I think it's better to regret *not* being a parent than it is to regret being one. The latter is pretty irreversible, unless you're one of these depressingly common absentee fathers who go out for cigarettes and never come back.)

Now, this is probably a good place to mention that I am not dense enough to believe that my own parents' divorce and my father's subsequent abandonment didn't play any role in my decision.

I'm sure this sounds dark, but I used to wish my father had been more like me. I wish he had been honest about not really wanting children in the first place, instead of going along with what he was "supposed" to do, without any consideration for the children who would have to live their whole lives knowing they were the result of a half-hearted decision . . . maybe even a *mistake*.

I've seen years' worth of photos of my childhood. I've studied my father's face. He looks so happy. He looks *just* like the pictures of my friends' husbands that flood my social media feed (as is usually the case in your mid-thirties). A man unable to hold back tears when he sees a positive pregnancy test. A calloused, gruff hand cupping the tiny, pink cheek of a newborn. Little doll-haired girls bouncing on their dads' shoulders. A man cheering loudly for his daughter as she makes her way around the bases of a softball field.

Sometimes when I'm scrolling through, I wonder which one of them will get in their car one day and never come back.

I'm sure that makes me sound like a terrible person, but what's worse is the damn near statistical certainty of it. According to the 2023 US Census Bureau, 17.6 million children (that's nearly one in four) live without a biological, step, or adoptive father in the home.

But since I'm not going to comment that under anyone's family photos, I just swallow it down and click *Like*, so as not to feel like a monster.

After my divorce, I knew that if I ever chose to be in a relationship again, my options would be limited. Because statistically speaking, most people *do* want (or have) children.

It was one of the first things I'd asked William on our FaceTime "date." I needed to know right off the bat because I wasn't going to budge, and I certainly wasn't going to deprive someone of their dream of parenthood by making them think that I might.

"I'm sure at some point I thought I wanted them," he said, "but I just don't have any interest now."

He said it so plainly that you could tell he'd never been grilled by the Mormons about it.

William and I had been on the same page from the start and it had been folded into a paper airplane headed who knows where. There was no biological clock on which to check the time. We would never longingly recount our life in stark befores and afters. The world was still our oyster, even if the pearls have tarnished a bit with age.

And yet, despite being perfectly content with just William and the dogs (and snakes!), there were still people who warned me regularly of the doomed nature of a childless life. Not only would it be purposeless, it would also render me incapable of knowing "a love like this," as parents often say. And you know what? *That,* I agree with.

I love my dogs more than life itself, but they didn't come complete with the ancient, raging hormones that course back and forth between a mother and a child she grew in her womb. So, if I had a child, yes, I probably *would* experience a "love like that"... but I don't have a child. I don't *want* a child. So, what does it matter? There's no sense in comparing the incomparable.

Regardless of who or what it is that we love, it's the same chemical process flooding our bodies with serotonin when we think of them. A picture of my dog means no less and no more to me than a picture of a woman's child does to her. The same exact signals fire in our brains when we see their faces. Love is so irrefutable that we can scan it, study it, document it in colors and frequencies.

The love I have for my dogs is the most powerful thing that *I've* ever personally experienced. To be honest, the idea that I could love something *more* than that actually scares me.

We can all only know what we've known, lost what we've lost, loved whom we've loved. We can only ever *truly* understand the paths we've taken, never the ones we didn't.

So no, I'll never know what it's like to have a baby. I'll never know what it's like to be a mom.

But one time, many years ago, I think I came pretty close. One time, many years ago... someone *did* call me Mom.

chapter thirteen

Mom

I was twenty-three years old when I was handed a seventeen-month-old baby.

Just two days before, my mother called to inform me that my brother's wife had collapsed, been airlifted to a hospital in San Francisco, and quickly diagnosed with acute promyelocytic leukemia. She was only twenty-six years old.

She and my brother had just had their first child together. A tow-headed, blue-eyed little boy named Wyatt. After a few days of sleeping on my brother's lap in a reclining chair in a hospital room, it was decided that Wyatt needed a stable place to stay. They didn't have much family in California. My mother was still back east in Connecticut. However, it was just a short plane ride from California to Salt Lake City where Neil and I had moved just one year earlier.

I'd held my nephew only once prior to that day he was placed in my arms. He had arrived via airplane, where he was handed off to me by one of his mom's relatives. He came complete with a diaper bag and a car seat, which I hooked up in my Jeep without issue. I'd babysat enough throughout my life to navigate that kind of gear.

On the way home, he was silent. So was I. What must he have been thinking? I found myself wondering if he could somehow smell that I was family... or if that was only a dog thing.

When I carried him and his single duffle bag of clothes into my 415-square-foot studio apartment, I felt... awkward. Like a Realtor showing an unimpressive property to a client.

Once inside the front door, there was a couch and a TV and a small opening in the wall where you could see into the kitchen, which was essentially a six-foot-long hallway.

Bucket and Dagwood, who were one and two at the time, emerged from the doorway that led to our bedroom, which was nothing but a full-size bed with five feet to spare until you hit the wall. Off of that room was a single bathroom, the only room in the entire residence with an actual door.

Neil and I had been living on an old sailboat just prior to this, but what had felt like luxury to us suddenly felt a bit cramped.

Wyatt was quiet, inquisitive, his blue eyes searching all around the room, sticky fingers reaching for Dagwood's golden fur. He steadied himself on his chubby little bowed legs as Bucket joined in to sniff the top of his head as Dagwood licked his cheeks. He'd been around dogs since he was born, so I wasn't surprised at how unbothered he was.

"This is your cousin Dagwood," I said, smiling, patting the top of his head.

"And that's Bucket." I motioned to the faded blue thrift store couch, from where she now sat observing us all. "She's probably not gonna want to hang out as much as Dags will, so . . ." I trailed off.

"And Uncle Neil will be home in a few days!"

I'd very quickly run out of ideas of what to say after that. I had spent so much time around children. I was *great* with children. But I was almost always on their turf, in their playrooms full of toys, where I could pick up some little action figure and start making funny voices and their moms would pop in to tell me all the things they liked and didn't like, which is very important when someone is too small to tell you that themselves. So Wyatt and I just sort of stared at each other, bewildered.

Eventually he toddled over to the coffee table, reaching for an (unlit) candle. He didn't cry when I took it away, rather moved on to poking the electrical outlets. I was going to have to babyproof this apartment posthaste.

Fortunately, we lived right across the street from a Target. The street, however, was four lanes wide with a speed limit of forty-five. My friends and I would sprint across it at night sometimes to grab munchies, but there was no way I was attempting that with a baby. Not to mention, he was shockingly heavy. "Dense" is how my mom described my brother as a baby, and I understood now why that was true for his son as well.

I shoved a spare diaper and a pack of wipes into my purse, because he had at least arrived with some of those handy. Then I bundled him up, clipped him into his car seat, drove forty-five seconds across the road, unclipped him from his car seat, and wiggled his little legs into the red shopping cart. He stared up at me with such calm curiosity, it was practically unnerving.

Pushing a little blond-haired babe around in a cart at Target shopping for diapers and toys and glass jars of pureed sweet potato felt like some alternate reality, as though I'd woken up that morning in a completely different life . . . as though the one I'd actually been living had all been just a dream. (Having out-of-body experiences at Target seems to be a recurring theme for me.)

By the time I got in line at the checkout, I'd grabbed a few toys, outlet covers, baby locks for the cabinets, and padded protectors for the corners of the coffee table so he didn't bash his head in while I wasn't looking.

An older woman cooed at him as he balanced on my hip, blue eyes peering over my shoulder at her. She smiled and asked how old.

"Two?" I said, as though *I* was asking *her*. "Pretty much two, I think." She raised her eyebrows before I hurriedly offered up that he was my nephew, at which she softened.

It was no surprise that everyone assumed he was mine. Not because he was some spitting image of me, but because this is Utah—the official Mormon headquarters—a twenty-three-year-old with a baby was beyond normal. It was practically expected. But this was the first time I was actually grateful to be surrounded by Mormons. Because if there's one thing they excel at, it's babies.

Coworkers brought me a high chair and a pack-and-play I intended to use as a crib and another box of toys, which was helpful because I had resorted to letting him smash the buttons on the DVD player just so long as it kept him from yanking on the electrical cords. One woman offered up a list of indoor playgrounds and children's museums. She said I could call her anytime.

My coworkers were probably relieved to finally have something in common with me, something they could carry on a conversation about. I'm sure I seemed more approachable with a baby on my hip.

Many of them steered clear when I strolled into the office with my iced coffee (Mormons can't have that) and my tattoo-covered arms, and, every now and again, the faint smell of a dive bar wafting off of me from the night before. I even left one day on a lunch break to get a tattoo on my middle finger.

I'd regale them with stories of what slot canyon I'd crawled through over the weekend, or what mountain I'd climbed with Bucket and Dagwood. I'd relay the horrors of trying to find a yellow cab company to take you home from a concert at midnight in *Utah*. (Rideshare companies like Uber didn't exist yet, mind you.)

I never tried to hide who I was, which was certainly nothing like them, but they kept me around because I think they—some not so admittedly—found it all to be pretty entertaining. Like I was some character from a television show they weren't allowed to watch growing up.

Perhaps the kindest gesture of all was that my boss offered to let me work from home while I was taking care of my nephew, which was pretty unheard of in 2013. I had to use a secure VPN to log in from my apartment as Wyatt repeatedly reached for the keyboard. Connecting to it reminded me of the old dial-up computer we had in my basement in the early 2000s.

homesick nomad

...

It was surprising how quickly Wyatt started calling me Mom.

He would get up from a nap or startle me awake at night from the pack-and-play shoved between the bed and the wall. So close, I could reach down and rub his soft head without even getting up. But some nights were harder.

"Ma!" he'd yell between choking tears. "Maa! Momm!"

"I'm here, honey, I'm here, it's okay," I'd whisper, picking him up, holding him to my chest. What was I to do? Correct him? Say, "No, Wyatt, I'm your Auntie Bri. Your mom is really sick right now..."

His language skills were mostly babbling and yelling, "No!" (He loved that one.) So, besides *Mom!* what other word does a seventeen-month-old know to call out when his little eyelids flicker open in the dark?

All I could do was hold him and rock him and let him call me Ma and promise him that he would see his real one again soon.

I remember that it happened on a Friday, because normally I would have been getting ready to go to a rowdy line dancing bar called the Westerner where my friend once won two hundred dollars cash in a bikini bull-riding contest (a mechanical bull, obviously).

Instead I was sitting on the closed toilet seat beside my bathtub, watching soap flying everywhere from Wyatt's singular bath toy: a little red tugboat that he would shake wildly or just throw clear across the bathroom.

I rested my chin on my closed fist and used my free hand to wipe the tears from my cheeks. I was trying to cry as softly and discreetly as I could. I didn't want to scare him. I also didn't want to leave the room, because the kid was in several inches of water.

Just a few minutes prior, he'd had what the childcare world refers to as "a blowout," which is essentially a diaper explosion that sends poop clear up the child's back. A full system diaper failure, if you will.

It was an astounding amount of poop. Maybe I'd been feeding him too many berries?

I'd been using a beach towel on the floor to change his diaper, so I dragged it into place with my foot as I held him out in front of me with rigid straight arms, trying not to breathe through my nose.

His diaper was so full that when I took it off and tried to roll it up, it just popped back open to reveal the whole mess inside. Wyatt's cries turned to high-pitched screams, which made the entire situation feel far more dire.

The commotion caused Bucket and Dagwood to come investigate, whereupon Dagwood stepped directly into the popped-open diaper and started spreading one shit-covered pawprint across the living room carpet.

"No! Dags! Fuck!! No no no no!"

Wyatt wailed even harder.

I had no choice but to deal with the carpet poop later because the poop on the now-naked child was far more pressing.

I shuffled into the bathroom, gently setting him down into the tub, spraying his whole body off with the showerhead, which he did not like at all.

Afterward, as I was filling the tub for what would hopefully feel like a regular bath, I realized I was out of any form of baby soap. The only options were a deep exfoliating body scrub, or an oatmeal-based skin soothing soap . . . for dogs. I'll give you one guess as to which one I used.

I watched through swollen eyes as bubbles flew past my face and onto the walls.

He was like a tiny tornado that came through my life out of nowhere. I'd barely slept, there was yogurt all over my shirt, and my car reeked of regurgitated apple juice. It felt like it had been ages since I'd done any of the things that made me feel like myself. Dirt roads and deserts called to me like a siren song. And perhaps most upsettingly, everything in my apartment was sticky, and now . . . covered in shit.

I slid down onto the floor and sat cross-legged beside the tub. His eyes always looked the bluest when he was blinking his own tears from them. Then he wrapped his chunky little fingers around the edge of the tub and peered at me over the porcelain with soap in his hair and water droplets on his nose. And he smiled. And everything stopped.

I was in the eye of the storm with this little person . . . this whole amazing little person. In no time at all, he completely uprooted everything I had known my life to be . . . but I was still madly in love with him, enraptured by him, mesmerized by him. For lack of a better description, it felt like Stockholm syndrome.

I reached my hand out and cupped his warm, wet cheek, and I think, for a moment, I understood something I never would have otherwise.

A couple months later, arrangements had been made for Wyatt to go back to California. We'd received the best possible news. His mom was given great odds of a full recovery. I couldn't imagine how much she must have missed him. Or perhaps, in the smallest way, I could now.

The morning after he left, I took a duffle bag and moved through the apartment methodically packing up the safety locks and the padded bumpers on the coffee table. I tossed in a few toys that he'd left on the kitchen floor and the baby books next to my bed. I was giving it all back to my coworkers (both the things they'd lent me and the ones I'd bought). I did one final sweep of the place before bringing the bag out to my car.

That night I treated myself to my favorite Thai place, lit some candles, and snuggled up on the couch with Bucket and Dagwood. I poured a glass of wine as the *Law & Order* theme song filled the room. I could play it as loud as I used to now that there were no bedtimes... no babies.

I was too tired to make it through more than one episode, so I settled on a nice hot shower before bed. When I pulled the shower curtain back, Wyatt's little red tugboat sat perched on the corner of the tub, right where he'd left it.

I picked it up slowly, carefully, cupping it with two hands as if it were made of glass. Then I held it to my chest . . . and I sobbed.

The time spent with my nephew didn't make me change my mind about being a mother. It just solidified how good I am at being an aunt. (The moment that was solidified for Wyatt was when I rented a Corvette to pick him up from school on his twelfth birthday.)

One day, he called for one of our regular chats, but he asked me something he never had before.

"Brianna, when are you going to have kids?"

"Whatttt?!" I said, playfully. "What the heck are you talkin' about?! *You're* my kid!"

He laughed, but asked again, more earnestly this time. "But are you gonna have a baby?"

I softened my voice to a whisper. "You're the only baby I'll ever have, Wy. You're the only kid who ever called me Mom."

"Good," he said back, satisfied.

He was too young to remember anything about the chaos he rained down on me that winter, but he still loves to hear the stories. His favorite, of course, being the one where I washed him with dog soap.

chapter fourteen

Twenty-Four Hours on the Low Road

William was the one who read it out loud to me, which made it worse in just about every way. It's surreal, after all, to have your new boyfriend read something written by your ex-husband on a Reddit thread that existed for the purpose of publicly humiliating you.

I'd gotten a text from a friend asking me if I was okay. That's all it said. Are you okay?

I knew immediately what it must have been pertaining to. I still hadn't told William the full extent of the Reddit harassment, despite the fact that the number of participants was now in the thousands. Not only because I was afraid he might read it all and decide they were right, but also because it felt so . . . juvenile. Like a child tugging on your shirtsleeve, crying, "Susie's being mean to me!" Because thus far, everybody had brushed me off as such, shooed me away as children tend to be when they're interrupting more *important* conversations.

I'd already been dealing with it for over a year and a half when we met. By then, the story was too long, but more importantly, too unbelievable. But there was no more hiding it now.

I was panicked and hysterical, so William grabbed the phone from me and read it silently before saying, "It's not crazy, he just sounds like he's blaming you, saying you're on drugs . . . but he did say he was the one who was driving when he hit Dagwood." He paused, then raised his eyebrows a bit.

"He mentioned me." He chuckled.

"What?!" I said incredulously.

"'Now she's dating some guy that looks like me in my glory days . . .'"

I stared at him, my mind racing, trying to settle on an emotion. All that I could muster was an overwhelming sense of embarrassment. Not for me necessarily . . . but for Neil.

It was a shocking and bizarre betrayal for him to have joined that page. In fact, if he hadn't posted a selfie to prove to the world that it was, in fact, him . . . I probably wouldn't have believed it. But there he was, smiling smugly, holding up a piece of paper with the date on it as if he were being kept in captivity and we all needed proof of life.

On it, he wrote that his participation on the page was "part of his healing journey," which might be one of the saddest, most misguided things I have ever heard.

I had accepted my fate as being someone who would never *really* escape the internet at this point, but I had given Neil every opportunity to. I used advanced settings on my Instagram to ban specific words. If you tried to type his name or even write "ex-husband" on any of my posts, your comment would automatically be hidden. To this *day*, I have never turned that setting off.

I scrolled back years and years and years and deleted every picture of him, even emailed a few companies asking them to remove photos of us from their websites.

I changed his name in my books, even though *everyone* who had followed me knew his real one. But it still didn't seem fair. Instagram was my choice, not his.

The profile he made on a dating app just a few weeks after I left, however, *was* his choice. It actually included a photo of *the two of us*. I knew right then he was not in his right mind. But he matched with a woman who had followed me (therefore, us) on Instagram for years prior to them "meeting." I used to wonder if he even knew that . . . but fortunately, taking care of him was no longer my problem.

What was *very* much my problem was the fact that his participation on the Reddit thread was like pouring gasoline onto a trash fire. His presence endorsed what these people were doing. It made them feel *justified* in doing it. Team Neil!!! they'd all post, like a bunch of preteens at a One Direction concert.

I think it was exciting for a lot of them to feel like they were a part of something . . . that they were in the actual orbit of folks they considered "famous." I can't imagine people who do this for fun have anything fulfilling or meaningful going on in their own lives.

But there were also a handful of people who posted about how *weird* it was that Neil was participating. Some even said that they were leaving the thread entirely because of it. Perhaps they had a temporary moment of humanity and realized this had gone beyond snarky, anonymous gossip . . . that this was, actually, really fucking dark.

Save for those few folks, the rest of the crowd grabbed their popcorn.

I might have tried to keep this huge, embarrassing, reality-TV-esque clusterfuck from William, but once Neil made that post, I knew I had to tell him everything. Up until that point, he probably assumed what everyone else did. That maybe I was just worried about a forum full of people saying I was ugly and stupid and the shittiest writer on earth.

But if that was all that thread had ever been, this isn't a story that you would be reading.

It started in 2020 when I came out with the truth about Dagwood's accident, just a few weeks after I had left Neil. At first it was just those fake accounts with names like *briannamadiaisadumpsterfire*. They even went so far as to make a fake LinkedIn account under my name that said I was "a professional scammer."

Then the emails started. Anonymous fake addresses that were just a smattering of numbers and letters smashed across the keyboard. One of them was from a woman claiming she had met Neil on a dating site just a few weeks after I'd moved out (who knows, maybe she had).

I had a great time fucking your husband last night, she wrote.

Any responses I sent to emails or comments or messages were immediately screenshotted and added to the thread so they could all celebrate how much they were getting me.

This sort of low-level (albeit, still awful) harassment continued throughout the fall of 2020 until I couldn't take it anymore. I took a few months' hiatus to try to keep myself from the edge they were so successfully pushing me toward.

During that time, I booked an appointment with my usual tattoo artist. The piece I was getting was the final scene of the movie *The Truman Show*, where Jim Carrey walks up the steps toward the exit door of a world that he just found out has been totally fake all along.

My artist, Megan, texted me that morning to ask if I wouldn't mind coming in a little early to say hello to the client she had before me. Let's call her Sandy. There were still Covid restrictions, so the shop was empty except for the three of us.

Sandy told me she was a *huge* fan. I told her I wished we were allowed to hug, because she was crying and her hands were shaking. She said she loved my Instagram and my dogs and had been following us for years and years. In fact, the only reason she was there was because I had tagged Megan on my Instagram after she tattooed portraits of Bucket and Dagwood on my arm.

I sat and talked with her for the remainder of her appointment. She shared a little about her life, and in turn, I did the same. It isn't my nature to hold back (I'm a memoirist, for God's sake), so I talked honestly about what I was going through at the time. This shocking divorce, my ex-husband's downward spiral. I even talked to her about the Reddit.

My tattoo artist was floored to hear the extent of what was happening online, but Sandy knew . . . just about every detail, even adding in ones I didn't know about. I should have known right then.

· · ·

When I came back online in early 2021, two months after meeting Sandy, it was obvious that she was a thriving member of the Reddit. In fact, she was one of few people on there who didn't even try to hide her identity.

This was a turning point in my life, not only because of what would follow, but because it was the first time that I realized what I had *actually* exposed myself to. Of course, I knew I was posting publicly to hundreds of thousands of people, but what I didn't consider is that it only takes *one* person to develop a frightening obsession. That was the first, but not the last time, that social media started to feel dangerous.

In early 2021, Sandy started contacting companies I worked with on Instagram, claiming that I was "distributing pornographic images of her."

Now, we all can sit here and say, *Who on earth would ever believe that some random influencer would be distributing pornography of a perfect stranger she met once at a tattoo shop?*

I thought the same thing. In fact, I laughed out loud when I heard what I was being accused of. But she continued posting step-by-step instructions for how to contact any company I was affiliated with. These would end up pinned to the top of the page for all the members to see.

The post instructed people to make a handful of fake accounts each . . . what to say . . . how often to call each company and say how "problematic" I was. (This was *the word* of the year because it was a great way to claim that someone was doing bad things without ever having to explain what those bad things were.)

Generally, when a photo of me was shared by any company, they were bombarded with comments from more fake accounts. She hit her dog and lied about it! and If you don't drop her, I'm never buying your products again!!!!

Brands I worked with sent me emails, one by one, saying they were going to have to end our partnerships. Many of them outright admitted that they *knew* the claims were fake. In fact, Backcountry actually put, in writing, that this was "a targeted effort on behalf of a small, coordinated group of people." They even offered to continue paying me under the table until "things died down." Until maybe they'd find someone else to go after.

But those anonymous accounts gave them enough of a headache on their social pages and customer service lines that it was easier for them to just drop me.

This was the height of cancel culture, and I was the fucking poster child for it. Both individuals and companies alike were terrified of being next.

Nulo Dog Food publicly tweeted that they were no longer working with me *before* they contacted me to tell me that. I found out I was fired on Twitter.

Thank you for doing the right thing!! faceless accounts would say beneath their retweets.

All of these things were always immediately posted to the Reddit thread, of course, and those folks just danced in the streets over it all. It worked! They were getting away with it! They felt *legitimized*, because those companies *legitimized* their behavior.

After the loss of my sponsorships, someone in the group contacted my publisher, urging them to cancel my book deal. They thought they were the first ones to tell them "the truth about Dagwood's accident," despite the fact that the *entire story* was included in the proposal for my book that had been accepted for publication almost a full year prior.

Regardless, the person who sent this message then actually sent a link for the Reddit as a "source of evidence" for my publisher to look over. A page where people with bizarre usernames like poopybutt123 called me a bitch and a fraud and an alcoholic and a liar . . . a subreddit where people thought it was fun to photoshop pictures of penises onto my face.

They actually viewed their blatant hate page as "proof" of something. They felt unashamed to send that to major companies . . . to one of the top five publishing houses in the entire country.

It's like if your name was John Green and someone emailed your boss a website called www.JohnGreenSucks.com and expected them to take that as an accurate source of unbiased information.

From there, it just got worse and worse. It was impossible to know who was doing what or how many people were doing it, but every day I woke up to something new. Hotels I was staying in received calls claiming I was doing drugs in the room. They posted my address, the phone numbers of my family members, the addresses of my friends' homes and their families' homes.

One evening, I was staying at an Airbnb in Salt Lake City when the owner called my cell phone. He said he got a long message from someone calling herself "Diane."

She wrote that my dogs were "tearing the place up" and "running loose on the property" and "killing the squirrel in the yard tree," and having a party where "multiple substances are being used."

Little did they know that the Airbnb was a duplex and the owner's parents lived downstairs, so they could confirm that this was all categorically false. The owner even offered to message "Diane" back and try to figure out who she was for me. I'd had to explain the saga to him as best as I could, which was (as it will always be) rather humiliating.

He felt so bad for me, he actually offered me an additional night for free, but I couldn't get out of there fast enough. I was convinced someone must have physically followed me, been hiding outside in the bushes. How else could they have found out exactly where I was?

As it turns out, members of the Reddit had spent that Friday evening searching through *every single* Airbnb in Salt Lake City to match up images of the house that they could make out in the snippets of my Instagram stories.

After that, I couldn't post anything in real time. I was clearly dealing with people who were so fixated, so *deeply* obsessed, that I no longer knew what they were capable of. And I was more afraid than ever to post anything about the Reddit for fear that it would send even more people to read it. A lot of times it did.

...

Another quick way to ruin someone's life in those days was to say they were racist.

At the time, so many people were paralyzed with white guilt that someone could just say "that person is racist," and boom, that person would be out of a job.

Don't believe me?

In April of 2022, my first memoir, *Nowhere for Very Long*, was set to be released. In the months preceding, members of the Reddit went onto the website Goodreads and left over fifty one-star reviews for it, claiming they had received some nonexistent early copy.

But! I had my *first-ever* book signing as a published author coming up fast, so I tried to focus on that instead. I'd spent weeks preparing, deciding which cowboy boots I would wear . . . which lucky hat (there's a few).

I'd dreamt of this for years.

Just three days before, the bookstore set to host my event abruptly sent an email out to the hundreds of scheduled attendees, saying that the event had been canceled.

To top it off, they also posted an announcement on their public Instagram page, which read

> Upon receiving some important feedback regarding the upcoming event with Brianna Madia, we have decided to cancel the event. We strive at all times to be an inclusive and safe space for everyone and will not amplify voices that don't align with our values.

This was news not only to me, but to my agent, editor, and entire publishing house. They contacted the bookstore immediately to ask what the hell was going on, to which the shop owner said, "Someone called and said Brianna is a white supremacist and that there would be a picket line outside the store if the event went on as scheduled."

My publisher's lawyers were on the phone with them so fast, their heads spun. But at this point, I realized I needed to get a lawyer of my own. That word *safe* struck me, took my breath away for a moment. They strive to be "a safe space." Were they actually insinuating—in writing—that I was a *danger to the public*?

I hired a defamation attorney in Salt Lake City and had him reach out to the bookstore, demanding evidence of what I was being accused of.

It seemed to dawn on them *only* then, that they had never been given a single shred. They said that a woman called the store and told them that, but said she was too afraid to give her name. My lawyer sat in stunned silence.

"Okay, was there a screenshot, or an email, or a documented exchange that supports the claim that Brianna is a . . . dangerous white supremacist?" he asked over the phone, as I sat with shaking hands on the other end of his long mahogany conference table. (As a result of all of this, I had now lost just about all of my income, so the lawyers' bills were now piling up exclusively on my credit card.)

Their response was completely unsurprising to me at that point, but my lawyer's jaw inched farther and farther toward the floor as he listened to the bookstore owner nervously stutter, "Well . . . she just called and said . . ."

That was it. That was all it took. A faceless, nameless person called their store and made a completely unsubstantiated claim, offered absolutely no evidence, and successfully destroyed what would have been my first-ever event as an author. I was—and always will be—*devastated* about that.

Given that Sandy was the only person whose *actual* name I knew, my lawyer could go after her. All I wanted was a public apology and for the Reddit page to be deleted. Those were the demands he sent.

But I never got that, because the moment the creators of the page heard that Sandy had a defamation attorney in her inbox, she was kicked out for "compromising the safety of their community."

Protecting their anonymity was the most important thing to them, because they *knew* from day one that what they were doing was wrong.

But what they didn't know—what so many people don't seem to even consider—is that you are anonymous on the internet . . . right up until you're not.

One afternoon, I got an email from a woman who called herself Selena. She said she didn't want to give her real name, and that's all it took for me to delete it immediately. The following week, she sent another email, which I also deleted without opening.

A few days later, I got a text from a friend of mine whose name was also mentioned on the Reddit thread.

Bri . . . she wrote, you're gonna wanna open that woman's emails . . .

Selena didn't know who I was before all of this. She said someone told her about this crazy Reddit that had gotten so out of hand, and after digging into it herself, she really just could *not* figure out what I had done to "deserve" it. Was it just that *my* husband ran over *my* dog? Was that what I had "done" to these people?

Apparently so, because they often referred to themselves as "victims" of mine. They said I had "personally victimized" each and every one of them. Perfect strangers . . . people whose names I didn't know, whose faces I couldn't even have picked out of a crowd . . . people who *chose* to follow me on Instagram for years on end now considered themselves "victims" of my mere existence.

But *I* was the victim. And Selena was the solution.

Attached to her email was an Excel sheet of names she had started to collect, completely of her own volition.

"These are some of the people on the Reddit," she wrote. "They're really not that hard to find, most of them use the same usernames to post things in other threads that are pretty identifying, sometimes even photos of their dogs that are identical to ones on their Instagram."

It took me a very long time to email her back and an even longer time to trust her, first because I didn't trust anyone, and second because I was confounded as to how she was able to do all of this.

"I'm a huge computer nerd," she said. "Finding these people is like a game with leads to follow and clues to put together."

Within a few months, I came to trust her so much that I gave her my Instagram log-in whenever she suspected she might have found someone's identity. She would like a post of theirs or, more often, block them suddenly and then go back to the Reddit to see if she was right about who they were. *Bri just blocked me! Hahahahahahaha!* they'd write.

Got 'em.

I wasn't the only one who came to trust Selena. She thought it would be a brilliant idea to *join* the Reddit (anonymously, of course) and spend months on end pretending to hate me. She'd often call me at the end of the day and say how sick it made her feel to have to write the things she was writing, but they had to believe she was "one of them."

Before long, she had worked her way up the ranks of that thread, gaining the trust of the other users, messaging them privately, gathering personal information about them. She even got some folks to just outright *give* her their names, which she promptly added to the list.

Eventually Selena had collected a *Law & Order* episode's worth of screenshots, messages, posts, photos, and email trails. She also used some sort of tech-savvy API server hacker shit that she tried (unsuccessfully) explaining to me, but I digress.

Ultimately, she presented me with a list of two hundred and thirteen names of the creators, moderators, and most prominently involved members of MadiaSnark.

. . .

I was a little surprised to find that Neil's oldest brother was an active member. I knew he never liked me very much, but he was a firefighter in Connecticut, in his mid-forties, with three grade-school-aged children. It was bizarre to picture this man I once knew coming home after a long day's work and choosing to spend his time speculating what drugs I was on, and gossiping with a bunch of random women who were hellbent on torturing someone he once sat around a Thanksgiving table with. How incredibly pathetic...

I wasn't surprised *at all* that Neil's oldest sister was also a member. She was a very, very strange person who never liked me to begin with and the feeling was extremely mutual.

Of course, Neil's name was on the list, along with a collection of things he had posted from his username, claiming he had "insider information about me."

Apparently that's when one of the moderators of the page—we'll call her Judy—from Flagstaff, Arizona, contacted Neil directly. They went so far as to exchange phone numbers, effectively making her the official "liaison" from my ex-husband and his siblings to the rest of the Reddit.

I cannot even begin to describe how surreal it is to find out that a total stranger from the internet has had a fucking conference call with your former in-laws.

After Selena sent me the list, I googled Judy's name and found a headshot of her from her website where she offered... "social media management" (you can't write this shit).

I spent over an hour googling names, scrolling through pictures, searching these peoples' faces for an explanation, for an understanding of how women who were nurses, mothers, teachers, *therapists*, for fuck's sake, could all be a part of this "community."

Because besides Neil and his brother, every other participant on that thread was a woman. Every. Single. One.

So you'll forgive me if my eyes roll out of my head and onto the fucking floor when women claim we're one big happy supportive sisterhood. Women can be absolutely vicious, especially when they're prisoners to their own internalized misogyny that tells them that someone who is successful, or bold, or audacious needs to be *put in her place.*

Who needs the patriarchy when you've got women doing their work?

Anytime I would even try to hint at what was happening to me, I'd be told no less than fifty times to "just ignore it."

No more income? Just ignore it!

People tracking your current physical locations? Just ignore it! Be strong!

You're being driven to the brink of what you feel you can live through? Take the high road!

When I couldn't just "be strong" and "ignore it," I felt like even more of a failure. I felt like I was screaming into a crowded room but no one was listening. It felt like no one cared. Those companies didn't care, that bookstore didn't care, all the podcasts that found this thread to be great fodder for their own content didn't care. The police department didn't care. (Yes, I literally called the Salt Lake City Police Department, though I prefaced the conversation with "I'm not sure if you can help me . . ." I felt embarrassed. Like a lost child who still believed that calling 911 was what you do when you're scared.)

But most importantly, both Reddit and Instagram didn't give one flying fuck, because *God knows* I spent entire days of my life requesting to have accounts deleted or threads taken down. Instagram denied my request to delete an account called @briannamadia isaplaguerat. They said it didn't qualify as harassment because I had a large public account. (What did I expect, right?!)

Reddit did nothing because Reddit has never done *anything* about the cesspool of hateful threads that their website is famous for.

I guess I didn't beg them for my life hard enough.

The only "solution" ever suggested was to *just ignore it.*

Take the high road.

A few months before I met William, "the high road" I considered taking was via a gun I'd bought at a sporting goods store. I planned to open my Instagram, start a live recording, press it to my temple, and squeeze the trigger. Give them one final screenshot to laugh at.

Maybe after I died, they would scroll back and see how many times I had asked for help. Maybe they'd pass some online bullying law so it wouldn't have been all for nothing.

Regardless, as soon as I was six feet under, I'd finally be able to ignore it.

I held on to that list of names for a very long time, unsure what to do with it, unsure if it was a can of worms I wanted to open. But one day, for no specific reason at all, I picked up my phone, opened Instagram, and spoke directly into the camera, stating that I had "hired an investigator" (if I said "an investigator volunteered," I didn't think it would sound as scary). I said we were able to find the identities of 213 of the most active users in the MadiaSnark subreddit thread.

Selena texted me almost immediately. She and I had discussed releasing the names before, but we were both adamant that the evidence needed to be overwhelming.

Are we doing this!!!? Are you ready!?

I responded immediately. What do I do, just start writing names??

Truthfully, I hoped making that statement would be all I'd have to do. Maybe that would be enough to scare them into deleting everything. After all, I'd been made to believe that the only way out of this was on the high road.

Selena's three little typing dots appeared, and then disappeared, then reappeared, then disappeared again. Instead, she sent a screenshot of a comment that had *just* been posted on the Reddit thread:

Do you guys really think she has 213 names? How is that even possible? Did she hire some FBI hacker? I don't know who any of y'all are, how could she? She also just directed her whole entire platform to this sub—again. Hi, new friends!!

I could feel my heartbeat in my temples as I watched Selena start typing again.

Post this screenshot and say, "Yes I do . . . Lauren."

When I think back, this moment feels like holding a match to the frayed tip of a fuse, watching as the first few sparks quiver to life.

Selena sent me another screenshot shortly thereafter. The comment had been deleted almost immediately. I stared in disbelief at my phone, unable to keep the corners of my mouth from curling up into a grin.

I held my breath, my palms sweating, the lit fuse crackling closer as I posted another screenshot of the now-*deleted* comment with big red letters across the top.

RUN LAUREN RUN!!!!!!!

Boom.

Within what felt like ten minutes, the internet went absolutely wild. Anonymous accounts from these bored, pathetic people are *rampant*, whether you're famous on the internet or not. I wanted people to see what happened when an entire industry, an entire society, lets it go completely unchecked . . . gives these people actual *power* from behind their curtains like some internet Wizard of Oz.

People were fucking tired of it. *I* was fucking tired of it.

Folks all over started sharing my stories where I had continued to attach names to screenshots of their vile comments, one after the other, after the other. Eventually, there was an average of one hundred thousand people viewing each and every slide.

> Here's Debbie making jokes about me killing myself. Debbie is a nurse, by the way . . .

> Here's Courtney celebrating getting me fired . . . hope no one ever does that to your young daughter.

> Here's April and Morgan whose last names are just riiiiiiighttt on the tip of my tongue . . .

Comments on the Reddit were being deleted left and right. People frantically tried to remove their usernames or make their Instagram accounts private. It was complete and total panic.

Now, mind you, Selena was still undercover on the Reddit as one of the "top dogs" so people started messaging *her* asking what they should do . . . freaking out about whether or not their identity was one of the ones found. Selena even managed to get a few *more* of their identities from these exchanges. (There's a reason I assume no one is going to believe me when I tell this story . . .) One of the messages she got was from Neil's brother. He was terribly worried that he might lose his job.

Sucks, doesn't it?

After the initial drop of *first* names only, mind you, I started receiving dozens of emails from people begging me not to release their information. Many of them had the exact same subject line: I'm sorry . . .

More than half of the apologies came from fake email accounts and started with something like, "I don't know if you have my name or not, but . . ."

More than half of them made mention of thinking of me more as a character on a show. Many even said that they "didn't think I would ever see any of it," which is an outright lie, given how many screenshots of me acknowledging this thread had been posted right there to begin with. But I would expect nothing less from people like that, or . . . nothing more, perhaps.

I never responded to a single one of those apologies, but I did spare the folks who used their real names from what happened next.

Bolstered by the encouragement I'd received thus far, I decided to record a full-length video, essentially telling this very story, but accompanied with screenshots and photos and irrefutable proof. You know what they say . . . If you fuck around, you might find out.

At the end of the video, I listed full names next to some of their most disturbing comments like rolling credits. Once again, the internet went *wild*.

I posted it on Instagram and YouTube, where it was collectively watched over *one million times*. I got requests for interviews left and right. People wanted to know who Selena was, how I had "hired" her. There were articles about it everywhere, including... the *Daily Mail*.

Podcasters all over were talking about it, including one that had spoken about the Reddit thread before all this. The episode was called "The #VanLife Influencer Who Flew Too Close to the Sun." I couldn't listen all the way through. I stopped after one of the hosts started laughing at the fact that I called 911 when Neil ran Dagwood over. "Who calls 911 for a dog?!"

That *very* podcast reached out to me via email, asking if I had any comment about my Reddit takedown. To which I responded:

> I'm familiar with your podcast. I heard the episode where you and your co-host laughed about me calling 911 when my dog was dying. I noticed you have a dog too. If, God forbid, Moose was ever hurt one day, 911 operators are always equipped with a list of local emergency veterinarians depending on where you're calling from. And while I have you, don't you ever let my dog's name slip out of your mouth again.

How's that for a fucking comment?

Another podcaster from *The Bachelor* called me "the Liam Neeson of Instagram" (à la his speech in the movie *Taken*: "I will find you... and I will kill you").

I certainly wasn't planning on killing anyone, but Selena turned out to be incredibly good at finding them. In fact, she had gathered so much information about these people, I could have included their horoscope and bra size if I wanted to. But I decided to post what I hoped would be enough for them to finally, *finally* stop. I stuck to names, occupations, and states. For example: Brian Madia, firefighter in Connecticut.

The fact that *so* many of these people had jobs in healthcare, had children, or worked with children was deeply disturbing to me, and felt pertinent to include for that reason alone.

If you've never experienced something like this, you probably believe you'd be able to recognize these kinds of people out in the world. You think you'd be able to see their horns. I wish I could tell you that was the case.

The majority of people fled immediately once the first name was dropped. What remained of "the community" began talking elsewhere on some other basement-dwelling website I'd never heard of. Only the most obsessed remained.

One woman decided she would contact the Utah State Bar and try to get them to revoke the license of my defamation attorney. They claimed he had assisted me in the criminal act of "doxxing," which is putting someone's personal information on the internet against their will. If you have more than two brain cells to knock together, you don't need me to explain the irony of that.

My lawyer's license was not revoked, of course, though he did get quite a kick out of the whole thing.

When it became apparent there was no legal route to take, a few folks talked of all kinds of plans to call all kinds of law enforcement branches, which I imagine would have gone something like this:

Hello, 911, the lady on the internet said that I said the things that I said.

They started coining the phrase "reverse bullying," which is literally just a weird way to admit that you know full well that *you* were bullying someone.

One woman posted that me sharing these people's names was causing "*real* harm." As if what they had spent three years doing to me wasn't "real."

Because to them, *I* wasn't real. What did I expect?

On camera, I tried to act tough and vindicated, but I'd collapse into William's arms at the end of each day, sobbing, robbed of every drop of strength I had left. In the morning, he'd hand me a cup of coffee, kiss my forehead, and say, "Give 'em hell, baby."

The main targets had always been the creators and moderators of the thread because they were the ones with the power to shut it down. And less than twenty-four hours after I told everybody who they were and what they had done . . . they did.

Selena was the first to tell me the news. I sat in front of my laptop with tears streaming silently down my face as William stood behind me, rubbing my shoulders. I typed *MadiaSnark* into the search bar and was met with a blank white page, a looking glass icon, and the words

> There aren't any search results for MadiaSnark, try checking your spelling.

It took me twenty-four hours to put a stop to the psychological warfare that had been systematically destroying my life for almost three years.

Fuck your high road.

There were a few hundred people on that thread who were so invested in hating me that it might as well have been their drug, Reddit their daily fix. But there were thousands upon thousands of other people who followed along. People who probably didn't take it *nearly* as seriously, who never left any comments themselves. I'm sure that to them, it was just gossip. Something to scroll through when they were bored on their lunch break.

They might not have been invested enough to know the extent of what that faction of people was actually doing, but their mere presence still makes them accountable. Because that smaller, dedicated, obsessive group was bolstered by numbers. Every follow, every upvote, every click cheered them on. It fueled them, emboldened them, allowed them to accomplish what they ultimately accomplished.

Those thousands of people may not have left any comments or

contacted any of my employers or had any conference calls with my former family members . . . but they were complicit. They watched in silence from behind a screen as someone suffered for years on end. Because that was *entertaining* to them.

Truthfully, I hate the lesson I learned from this. I hate that the high road doesn't seem to work as well as we once thought. But desperate times call for desperate measures.

There is an epidemic of this behavior on the internet and hell will freeze over before I tell my nephew to ignore anything of the sort. Because we are telling the wrong people to ignore it. People like me wouldn't have to fight so hard to ignore the cruelty, if those doling it out had just ignored *us* in the first place. At no point was it a government mandate to follow me on Instagram. If *they* had just ignored *me*, none of this ever would have happened. Over a million people would never have seen their names alongside proof of who they *really* are.

You can take the high road or the low road or drive right off a cliff for all I care, but at the end of the day, what you think of a stranger on the internet is not their responsibility.

So . . . ignore it! Take the high road *or* take the risk.

If you want to spend your one precious life in these seedy internet corners, stewing in vitriol, you be my guest. Just don't ever say I didn't warn you. You are anonymous on the internet right up until you're not . . . right up until you're being written about in a book.

chapter fifteen

Exit 241

My friend Katie told me that it's nothing like it once was. Few things are, I suppose.

She said it's practically unrecognizable with the number of people, the posted campsites, the paved bridges, the whining of dirt bikes and ATVs. For me to go out there now would be akin to driving past your quaint childhood house to find it had been turned into a shopping mall.

I can't pass the exit without the muscle memory kicking in. *Turn the wheel. Go home.* But I never do. It's been over half a decade since I've heard the click-click-click of my right blinker like a quickening heartbeat as I slipped off the freeway, passing the lone gas station on the corner of this tiny town that seemed to house only a few folks who had never found their way out.

It was a relatively desolate place, but that's how I preferred most places.

A few houses and a handful of churches later, you're spit out onto a sun-bleached, two-lane road surrounded by open range cattle and roadkill roasting on the pavement. Eleven miles after that, from seemingly nowhere, another little town appears. And in that tiny desert town, just past the single blinking stoplight, is a left turn out into a place called the Swell.

There's a post office just shy of that dirt road that served as the only "address" Neil and I had at the time. Mailing only. Because *home* was Bertha. And we'd blow past that post office and head straight for that dirt road because we were young and wild and totally irresponsible and deeply uninterested in whatever real-world paperwork was piling up in there.

That one left turn was our hundred-mile-long driveway out to the quietest canyons, the deepest walls, the bluest skies. The mule deer would peek out from behind the cottonwoods as dust from our tires plumed up around them like the early morning fog.

Chalk-white piles of bones dotted the dried, open fields, a reminder of how harsh our version of paradise could be.

In the summer months, we'd always park beside the same muddy, knee-deep river. It was low enough to be able to plop my camp chair down directly in the center of it. From there, I could still see the tops of the towering red buttes above the swaying of the Indian grass while crawdads squirmed beneath my toes.

Bucket and Dagwood grew up out there. They were as much a part of the landscape as the beavers they so diligently patrolled the shores for. Besides Bertha, that stretch of solid ground was the only thing that felt like home. Sure, we ventured all over the deserts and mountains of the American West (Utah especially). But of all the places, that one felt like it belonged only to us.

And then, one day, there was no more us.

In the beginning, I was embarrassed to be divorced at just thirty years old. Out of curiosity, I googled the national statistics one day, only to find that the average age of couples going through their first divorce is, in fact, thirty years old.

Regardless, I didn't personally know any other divorced thirty-year-olds. I knew engaged people. I knew pregnant people. I knew people posting photos of themselves holding the keys to their first house. Everyone's life was moving along while I'd been bumped back to *start* on the board game.

It didn't help that the whole saga had been dissected across the internet like an NFL postgame show. Or that you can't swing a cat without hitting some article about the divorce rates nowadays. "Marriages used to last!" they say. To which I've always wondered, *Yes, but were they happy ones?*

Because, mind you, it was only 1974 when the Equal Credit Opportunity Act granted women the right to have their *own* bank account. I'm sure plenty of wives would have loved nothing more than to slap their no-good husband and burn rubber down the driveway, holding up a middle finger all the while.

Things were different back then, sure, but different doesn't mean better.

homesick nomad

· · ·

Being divorced only felt like a failure until I started asking myself what "succeeding" would have looked like. Staying in that marriage no matter what I had already put up with? No matter what I'd have to keep putting up with?

When we exchanged vows on that hillside in Connecticut, I *truly* believed we'd be one of those couples in the local newspaper, clutching hands, celebrating seventy years of marriage, but newspapers probably won't even exist by then, so I try not to worry about it.

What should matter more than the length of the marriage is the quality of it. Does it sustain and support and encourage the best parts of you? I'm sure, in all relationships, there was a time that it did. And if that really does last all the way up to a newspaper article, that's amazing. And if it doesn't, just remember, there is nothing impressive about staying unhappy.

Sometimes I think I left Neil as quickly as I did because I didn't want us to spend months, years turning into those people who absolutely fucking *despised* each other. That felt like the only way to preserve the memories I still loved.

I couldn't stick around and watch it devolve into something I wouldn't be able to unsee, images that would permanently override the way I wanted to remember him and the third of my life that we'd spent together.

Because I'm not an open casket person. I refuse to look at the frail, pallid remains of a person or a place I once knew and loved.

Perhaps it sounds strange, but nowadays, I try to think of my marriage in the same way that I think of the Swell. I try to remember it for what it once was. It's not always easy, especially given Neil's absolutely stunning betrayal . . . but I try. Because changing your perspective is tedious and exhausting, but not nearly as exhausting as anger.

I don't see it as avoidance. I see it as preservation.

A museum display, frozen in time behind thick glass with a painted bluebird sky and little taxidermized lizards and jackrabbits all frozen in place. As if time had stopped forever on a perfectly beautiful day, sparing them from knowing how it all ends.

chapter sixteen

Gone. Missing.

I am somewhere down a dirt road, as I almost always am. On the front seat of my Jeep is the ever-present layer of dried mud and dog hair and an old faded map of Utah. There's something so romantic about a paper map. It sits up on the dash, fading in the sun no matter where I am.

There's also my camera and a cooler with a bottle of wine. I always thought it would be sexier if I liked beer, but I just don't like beer. I'd like to tell you there's a handful of meals in that cooler too, but it's probably just a Tupperware of cold noodles and a few granola bars. Appetites are often fleeting in triple-digit temperatures.

In the glove box is a paperback copy of *Women Who Run with the Wolves*, the one whose pages are still water-warped from the tears I cried down onto them when I was alone in Mexico on my thirtieth birthday, murmuring the word *divorce* out loud for the first time.

In the back seat there's four dogs, who now ride on a fancy new platform that William built for them. It's level with the windows and the perfect shape for the massive memory foam bed they share like the true pack they are.

Now I can shove my rolled-up paddleboard *beneath* the platform, along with a few backpacks and blankets, and sometimes a tent. But sometimes, fuck it, we'll just cowboy camp.

On the passenger side floorboard is one of my busted up, five-gallon water jugs. The same ones I've been carting around for the past ten years. I like to joke that they're what I got custody of in the divorce. A couple of those blue jugs, one old orange van, my snakes, my dogs, and total freedom. I made out like a bandit, wouldn't you say?

It's remarkable how much your definition of a word can change throughout all the years in which you've used it.

Crowded to me, as a teenager, wasn't just a measurement, it was a requirement. The more crowded a party was, the better. The more kids packed into a school dance, the more worthwhile the whole thing was. Growing up forty-five minutes outside of New York City meant that I was used to being packed in like sardines with everybody else. Close enough to peer through each other's windows, pick through each other's trash.

By the time I drove down to Baja nearly two decades later, *crowded* to me had become one single plume of dust from any vehicle that wasn't mine. Most often, it was just one of those surly, mustached ranchers out to check on their cattle. They'd pass by, giving a single nod from the tip of a cowboy hat while the dogs voiced their warning. Whether in Utah or Baja, those folks aren't usually the chattin' type, so if I have to cross paths with anyone, it's them I prefer.

But more often than not, it's just us out there. Just the way we like it.

My plan was simple. Essentially, I intended to repeat the solo trip I'd taken with the dogs that summer in 2021. The summer that I met William.

Only this time, I'd be heading down in late November when the weather was cooler. Most people, including William, prefer this. I do not. However, I will concede that it's nice to know the sand won't ever be too hot for the dogs' paws.

The previous two years, we'd gone to Baja for the winter together. He was able to rent his house out to some travel nurses, who were miraculously not afraid of snake-sitting Bean and Mae.

Baja was what William and I had in common from our very first conversation. It's where we "met," where we got engaged, where we started our first holiday tradition. We'd find a dollar store and split up, eyeing each other suspiciously from the corner of the aisles. The task was to pick a Christmas present, but we couldn't risk the other person seeing it before we unwrapped them in the parking lot two minutes later.

William got me a little plastic dog figurine. I got him a spoon.

. . .

Despite the fact that this had become *our* place, it had first been one of mine. I decided that the dogs and I would drive down for a few weeks, and then William would *fly* down for a week to spend Christmas with us. Then me and the dogs would spend another few weeks bumming around before heading back up toward the border.

When he kissed me goodbye in his driveway, I'm sure he thought it was just another one of my regularly required independent adventures . . . but there was something rooted deeper in this one. I needed to prove to *myself* that I could do it again, that I could be as fearless as I'd been the first time around. I needed evidence that my bravery wasn't just a side effect of my grief. That the risks I took were because I loved living this way, not because I no longer cared to live at all.

But the moment I crossed the border, it was like no time had passed. There was no doubt in my mind that I was still the woman I hoped I'd be.

The first few weeks weren't unlike my first solo trip, save for a few more folks on the roads and the water being too cold to float in for very long (at least for me; Bucket was still as happy as ever). We visited all the same beaches, all the same quiet spots, and a few new ones too. I even rented the same Airbnb I'd stayed in with the FaceTime-capable Wi-Fi, so William and I could reenact our "first date."

I was in all of the same places physically, but in a profoundly different one mentally. It's terribly cliché to wax poetic about how time heals, but sometimes clichés exist for a reason.

It was the day before Christmas Eve when I checked into the

little white single-room, dome-shaped house I had booked on a cliff overlooking the Sea of Cortés. The roads to get out there were treacherous, even by my standards, but that only serves as a filter for keeping more folks away.

As I pulled in the driveway, a woman and her young daughter stood waving. She had a mop and a bucket of cleaning supplies, which reminded me that the owner had sent a message saying the cleaning lady would meet me to give me the keys and show me the house.

She spoke no English, so the tour commenced in Spanish. Usually, I just politely nod and smile at folks as they speak to me in languages I don't understand. But I startled the cleaning lady by shouting "basura!!" like an overly enthusiastic kindergartener when she pointed at the garbage can beneath the sink.

I could scarcely speak *back* to her, but for the first time, I found myself nodding with a genuine understanding. The fact that she was pantomiming things was helpful, of course, but I would catch multiple words that I knew, murmuring each one out loud in English immediately after she spoke it.

"Por la noche"—*night!*—"mantenga las ventanas"—*windows!*—"cerradas, por favor." *Please!*

There's a reason most teachers will tell you that the fastest way to learn a language is to just go throw yourself into the middle of it. Each time I would get a word right, the cleaning lady would enthusiastically sing, "Siiiiiii!" *Yes!* "Muy bien!" *Very good!*

The next day, I drove two hours to the lone airport in the bustling, drunken resort city of Cabo San Lucas where William would be waiting. That's the only place that *doesn't* feel like Baja to me, so we didn't stay long.

When we arrived at the cliff house, I attempted to give him the same tour in Spanish. He didn't understand much of it, probably because I was speaking mostly nonsense. But I like to think the cleaning lady would be proud of my efforts.

I hung up six Christmas stockings on the old wooden porch overlooking the water, and wrapped a string of twinkly lights around the banister. For days, we sat on the beach, seeing nothing but sand and water and joyful dogs and a constant spray on the horizon from the blowholes of the gray whales that travel twelve thousand miles from the Arctic every year to mate.

I would read in the sun and wander with the dogs while William went out spearfishing, emerging from the water with an armful of snappers, yellowtails, and sometimes wahoos.

He would clean and fillet them right at the water's edge, tossing the skin and other bits back into the ocean, where the seagulls circling above would dive for them headfirst. Banjo and Birdie kept a close watch on the fish bits *and* the gulls, not sure which was more worth their time.

Dagwood would often appear on some overlook somewhere, looking out toward the sea in that wise, all-knowing way that he does, while Bucket pranced up and down the beach on limbs you'd *never* suspect belonged to a thirteen-year-old dog.

In the evenings, we'd chop up some cabbage and avocado for

fresh fish tacos, eating them on the deck over the sound of the waves. Each day was the same, but I loved it even more because of that.

After William left, I spent another week and a half bouncing from beach to beach with the dogs before going back down to Cabo to pick up two friends who flew in for my birthday.

On the evening before they were set to fly back out, I awoke to the sound of Alice violently retching into the toilet of our Airbnb. When I stood to go check on her, I could see that Dagwood was having some issues of his own.

When his stomach gets upset, he has the tendency to . . . leak.

The nerve damage from the accident weakened his sphincter muscles, and the aging process didn't help. When he was going through one of his bouts, William would cover all of the couches and beds in his house with old sheets, knowing that I'd never banish him to the floor, no matter the circumstances.

I'd just follow him around the house with wet wipes, and every once in a blue moon, if he was *really* leaky, I'd slide a diaper on him while he slept overnight.

He never protested, but I still hated it. I tried to focus, instead, on the fact that the initial prognosis all those years ago was that I would be changing his diapers every day for the rest of his life. Only needing them every now and then was still a miracle.

What was also a miracle was that, due to a total lack of tail, Dagwood was able to wear human diapers, which, believe it or not, are *cheaper* than dog diapers. Not to mention, there is nowhere on the *entire* Baja peninsula that would sell dog diapers.

I stopped at a supermercado after I dropped off poor Alice at the airport. She was still yellow and slicked with sweat but finally void of anything left to throw up.

They didn't have baby diapers in a size big enough for Dags, but they did have adult diapers in a nice, sensible beige color, which I thought would blend nicely with his fur so he wouldn't be embarrassed.

Back in the parking lot, I opened the Jeep to find an absolute crime scene. Dagwood had pooped onto himself, the bed, and effectively all three of his siblings. They might have been a little mad at him, but I could never be. I had begged every doctor, every deity I could think of to let me keep him. I'd clean out a poop-covered car every day of the week if I had to, so long as Dagwood was in it.

At a gas station beside a boiling hot dumpster, I used an entire container of Clorox wipes on all the surfaces and baby wipes for all the dogs, comforting them throughout.

I might be a deeply scattered and often unprepared person, but when you have four dogs, these are things you always, *always* have on hand.

"I'm sorry, Banjo, it's just this one paw. He can't help it, and we love him so much, right?"

"It's okay, baby," I said to Dags, while bent over just six to eight inches from his butthole. "It happens, buddy, we'll get it all sorted. You'll be good as new in a day or two. Good as newwwww in a dayyyy or twoooooo," I sang, scrubbing the back of one of his legs.

A group of local workers sitting beneath a shady tree eating their lunch looked on in disbelief. I think I saw a chunk of apple fall out of one of their mouths as they watched me slide Dagwood's butt into Baja's version of Depend adult diapers.

I flipped the poop-covered bed upside down onto an old towel so the dogs could still lie on it for padding while we drove to our next Airbnb, which most likely did not have a washer and dryer, because that's scarcely a thing in the kind of places I stay. It's not like Ritz-Carlton-level establishments welcome four dogs (one in a diaper) with open arms.

By the time we arrived, I assumed my queasy stomach was from being engulfed in the lingering smell of dog shit for almost an hour, but as soon as I made it inside, the bathroom was the first place I headed.

I cannot even begin to express the absurdity of this house's architecture, but it plays a role in this story, so I will do my best. The front door opened into the living room, where the walls were as red as the lipstick the little boy used to write REDRUM on the door in *The Shining*.

The ceiling was fifteen feet tall and there was not one single thing hanging on the walls. There were a few small windows, however they had nary a blind, shutter, curtain, or even just a sheet pinned to the wall like the guy I dated in college used to do.

There were no rugs or carpets anywhere in the home. Nothing but wall-to-wall white floor tiles. Between that and the towering ceilings, every word I spoke had a significant echo.

Off to the right of the single leather love seat in front of a nearly floor-to-ceiling flat-screen TV was the kitchen, which was also redrum-red.

I assumed it was because it was technically part of the same room, but was also not surprised to find the bedroom had been painted the same color.

There were no blankets on the bed, just one military-tucked sheet on top of the *tallest* bed frame I have ever seen in my life. At five foot ten, I still needed a running start.

Perhaps most interestingly, the entire base of the bed was one huge block of dark wood. So large, in fact, that it looked more like some kind of altar. The mattress itself didn't even come close to the edge on any side. It was positioned in the middle like the yolk of an egg.

In the kitchen, there were no bowls, only plates. No forks, only spoons. This didn't matter much, because the idea of eating something was *absolutely* off the table at this point.

But most importantly . . . there was no water.

Every Airbnb, even the seedy ones, provides drinking water. It's how everyone—locals included—drink clean water. In the bigger towns, fancy people can even have it delivered right to their door. Cars full of gigantic blue jugs of it patrol the streets like ice cream trucks.

And yet, despite drinking water being everywhere else . . . it was not here.

I decided I needed to lie down before I attempted to deal with this issue. I had what remained in my water bottle for the moment, but things declined rapidly as soon as I made it up onto my ritual sacrifice bed. I was no longer convinced I'd escaped whatever bug had nearly taken Alice out.

I slept for as long as my stomach would let me, but when I climbed down from the bed, I lost vision entirely. I braced myself against the wall, but I couldn't wait there long. I stumbled like a drunk *all the way across the house* because that was where the one and only bathroom was.

The bed and the toilet could not physically have been farther away unless you put one of them outside. By the time I made it to the middle of the living room, I dropped to my knees, knowing I was going to pass out, and not wanting to land face first on the marble floor.

I opened my eyes—who knows how long later—to the dogs frantically licking me. I had a purple lump on the top right corner of my forehead . . . and I no longer needed to get to the toilet, as the toilet had become my pajamas.

I crawled on hands and knees past the kitchen island, which was almost as tall as the altar I'd been lying on. The shower was a small tiled square with a limp white curtain that covered one-third of it at most.

I reached up and turned the water on, which came out in such a depressing trickle that for a moment I thought the owner had forgotten to pay the water bill. Every drop looked like it was going to be its last. And every drop was absolutely *freezing*.

The water never got stronger or hotter, but I had no other options, so I crouched in there naked and crying and puking. By the time I felt safe enough to crawl out, my lips were blue, my fingers numb.

I staggered back toward the bedroom but dropped to the floor when my vision started to go again. My bony knees bruised against the tiles as I resumed crawling past Dagwood who was asleep, enjoying the coolness of said tiles. It occurred to me then that I hadn't checked his diaper in a while. My hands were still numb and shaking as I pulled it back to peek inside, thrilled to find that it was still clean.

At least one of us was getting better.

That's when the idea came to me. This was, hands down, the sickest I had ever been in my life. There was no way I was going to make it back and forth between these rooms all day. So as a contingency plan, I slid on a sensible beige diaper too. "We match," I whispered, as I lay with my cheek to the floor beside him, still shivering violently, but too tired to move.

I don't know if I fell asleep or passed out, but when I opened my eyes, I was still on the floor and now overcome with a panicked thirst. What remained of my water bottle had been drunk and then thrown up into the shower drain. I had nothing.

Miraculously, there was Wi-Fi at this place, but an occasional text was all I could get out. Even if I could call someone, what could they do? I didn't know a single person within three thousand miles of me.

I tried to get texts out to William when I could, but when my phone battery started dying, the only outlet in the bedroom was, you guessed it, on the complete opposite side of the bed on a wall that had no furniture, given that the bed was the only piece of furniture in the entire room.

At one point, I considered calling an ambulance, because I truly believed I had cracked one of my ribs from the vomiting, and then the nonstop dry heaving when there was nothing left to vomit. But I refused to leave the dogs.

I convinced myself that if I could just get water, I would be okay.

I remembered passing an Oxxo (Baja's version of a 7-Eleven) on the way into the neighborhood, so I thought, since I had regained the ability to stand up, that I could walk there. I gripped the banister down the stairs and reached out to grab the corner of the stucco building.

The next thing I remember is waking up, facedown, with a mouth full of dirt . . . that I still had no water to rinse out. When I crawled back upstairs, I sucked in a mouthful from the sink because at that point, I didn't think it would be possible to get any sicker.

I tried to send messages to the owner through the Airbnb app, but they went unanswered.

I texted William and told him I was scared. And that made him *really* scared. He wanted me to call an ambulance too. But I wouldn't.

I remember wishing I could just hear his voice. All I wanted was to hear his voice, instead of my own labored breathing. I lay shivering and crying beneath my singular sheet, wishing more than anything that he was there to call me "baby."

Fuck it, I would have even let him treat me like one.

. . .

I couldn't tell you what time it was or how long I'd gone without water when the dogs started barking. There was someone outside on the steps. Frantically, I crawled to the door and opened it, sending the dogs running down the stairs toward an older woman with a bucket of cleaning supplies.

She froze, her eyes widening, but the dogs blew past her, much more interested in the neighbor dogs who were hanging out on their roof. Her eyes got even wider when she saw me on the ground, reaching up at her like some zombie movie.

"Agua? Tienes agua?" I said, my lips cracked and sticking together. "I'm so sick," I said (because I didn't know how to say that in Spanish). My voice cracked when the words came out. She said something back to me, as she turned and walked back down the stairs, but I didn't understand. The soft tone of her voice was the only thing that made me think she might come back.

Not too long after, there was a knock at the door, which I dragged myself over to slowly. Slow enough to only catch the final flash of her dark curly hair as she rounded the bottom steps.

On the ground was an Oxxo bag filled with water and Gatorlyte and crackers and what I assumed to be some form of Tylenol.

I crouched over it, in tears, despite how much worse the crying made my headache.

It took me two days to be able to leave that Airbnb.

Fortunately, the owner did finally bring me drinkable water, but I was too afraid to eat anything. I was still weak and exhausted by the time I hauled my bags down the stairs, trailed by the dogs, who were also moving slower than usual. They could sense I still wasn't myself.

When I rounded the corner, I could see the imprint in the dirt of where my face had hit the ground. I had another week of wandering planned before I started the multiday drive back to the border, but I threw all of it to the wayside and booked it straight to Bend.

I'd always thought I understood what it meant to feel truly alone—no backup plan, no one to turn to. But apparently, I hadn't. That experience rattled me so deeply that I spent the entire drive north fantasizing about bursting through the front door straight into William's arms. I wanted to feel small. Safe. I was homesick for him *and* those four walls.

It was startling to find myself *missing* anything at all, let alone a house in the suburbs. For a long time, the idea of missing something felt dangerous. Missing something meant you cared enough to feel its absence. Missing something was a crack of light through the doorway that took more bravery than you'd like to admit to open in the first place.

chapter seventeen

Bertha

Everything I know about auto mechanics, I've learned against my will.

That is to say, when you own a van that's been breaking down regularly for an entire decade, you eventually learn about the whole rusted, oil-leaking operation whether you wanted to or not.

It started with me frantically googling things in the front seat in 2017 while Neil was beneath the van on the side of some lonesome freeway in South Dakota.

I think I typed *What makes a tire fall off your car?*

From there, I learned that Bertha's tires were connected to the axles via wheel spindles on either end that sort of "screw in" to the wheel hub as part of her suspension. They were likely snapping due to the pressure of her *massive* E-350 van frame being custom welded onto an F-150 pickup truck chassis from the 1970s. (I also had to google how to pronounce *chassis*.)

homesick nomad

When Bertha wouldn't start (one of her more popular magic tricks), I learned to understand how cars *do* start.

At the most basic level, you need three things when you turn the key: air, fuel, and a spark. From there you can start to narrow it down. If she's not turning over at all, you've likely got an electricity issue. If she's trying but can't turn over, could be airflow or fuel pressure.

I learned the difference between the colors and viscosities of all the various fluids that might begin leaking out of her at any moment. Eventually I learned the different smells too, since they were often embedded in my skin, deeply discoloring my nailbeds until I could get myself to the next rest stop sink.

Perhaps most importantly, I perfected describing things to mechanics over the phone from out in the middle of nowhere. Because believe it or not, there's a very important difference between a "clunking" sound versus a "knocking" sound. There's a difference between a squeak and a grind, a rough idle and a surging engine. After ten years, this had become Bertha's language. So I had to figure out how to speak it.

I learned the ins and outs of that van breakdown by breakdown, as though Bertha was holding up flash cards to a toddler with pictures of car parts on them. *The thing that just violently fell off my underbelly onto this dirt road? That's called theeee... driveshaft! That's right!*

I know what you're thinking. *Just get a new fucking van, lady.* I know what you're thinking because I've thought it too. It feels sacrilegious to admit... but I have.

. . .

It was spring of 2025 when I packed up Bertha to head down to Utah for two months. William helped me organize things, despite both of us knowing it would just devolve into an absolute mess a few hours into the trip. He also did the obligatory scan of Bertha's underbelly and engine compartment. He was readying the runway so that the dogs and I could fly.

It made me smile, even though it was something I once struggled with. But I'd come to understand that if someone wants to help you, it doesn't always mean that they think you're incapable. It might just mean that they love you.

Two months was a short trip, given that I had lived in that van for years on end, but it made me feel all the same old feelings again. I bought Bertha back in 2016. And here I was all these years later, shoving bags of clothes and cowboy boots and dog food and boxed wine into a thirty-five-year-old van. A van the very same age as me.

Living in Bertha in my late twenties meant my life was different than the lives of most folks I knew. It was most *certainly* different from all the folks I grew up with in Connecticut. But announcing that you're moving back into your van—even if only for a short while—feels even *more* out of the ordinary when you're in your mid-thirties. As if that's the type of thing I should have outgrown by now.

In all my group chats with friends, I'd slide in between photos of home renovations and invites to baby's first birthday parties with the revelation that I was going out to reclaim my #vanlife glory days.

They greeted it with the unmatched enthusiasm I always receive from the people who truly love me, but when Bertha's ignition switch went out the very morning that I was scheduled to set south, I found myself feeling too foolish to tell anyone.

By 2025, I had easily spent close to six figures on that van during the nine years in which I had her. If that sounds insane, it's because it is. From the outside, my love for Bertha probably looked more like a toxic relationship that I refused to break off.

After spending two hours figuring out what was wrong with the ignition switch, I finally got on the road, where I proceeded to spend the next hour convinced that there was something wrong with the engine. It took me almost to the Idaho border to remember that that's just how Bertha's engine sounds. That's really just how loud she is.

As we hummed along through the wide-open fields, I found myself overcome with a wave of pride. To this day I can hardly believe that twenty-six-year-old me just . . . climbed up into the driver's seat, cranked the key, and felt that behemoth thing shudder to life.

I had never driven anything even remotely like that before. And here I was again, being humbled by the same van that had pretty much done nothing *but* humble me since that very day.

I'd forgotten how loud she was, but I never forgot how much attention she gets. Stunned amusement is the best way to describe the looks I get from folks flying past us, especially given the most recent addition I'd slapped to her front grille.

Positioned perfectly around her custom emblem that once said FORD, but now says BERTHA, is a pair of thirty-five-inch-tall kudu horns. So large, in fact, that the top ten inches stick out above her snub-nosed hood. Through the windshield, she looks like some kind of mythical creature whose back you're riding on.

Not only are the horns huge, they're also very clearly *not* from around here. Kudus are large antelope with grayish-brown coats and distinctive symmetrical spiral horns. They're known as the "gray ghosts of the African bush."

I learned that from a woman at an antique shop on the side of the road in South Africa. The horns were tucked in the back corner (the best things usually are) lying flat on an old wooden tabletop. They were still attached to a triangle piece of skull that held them together, but they weren't mounted or preserved in any way.

She charged me fifty bucks for the free roadkill, and threw a wave as I hauled them up the stairs onto the bus. I hadn't the slightest idea how I was going to get them back to the US, but I had a few more days of the trip left to figure that out.

I settled on a huge flat-screen TV box that I'd found at a moving store in Cape Town. William and I crawled around the shop floor on hands and knees, wrapping the horns in as much Bubble Wrap as they had in stock. Then we slid them into the box and shoved the rest of the dead airspace full of even more Bubble Wrap.

The plan was to check the box as "oversized luggage" as opposed to paying some astronomical fee to ship them. We were flying back from South Africa to a tiny airport in Baja, Mexico, where we had put William's sister up in an Airbnb so she could watch the dogs. We still had another month left of our winter voyage down there.

At the oversized baggage claim area (a.k.a. on the floor near a single customs desk) was my box. The horns made it unscathed, much to my delight, but we hadn't considered that I'd have to fit that box into what was already a *very* packed van. So, believe it or not, strapping kudu horns to Bertha's front bumper with wire and zip ties started out as a logistical solution. Before I knew it, I could scarcely remember her without them.

I don't usually have time to say all of that when people come up to ask about them at various gas stations and grocery store parking lots. Usually, I just clarify that they are kudu horns from South Africa and I didn't kill the kudu myself. (This was a question I didn't think I'd be asked as often as I am, but that's the American West for you, I suppose.)

Bertha may have been back on the road, but the nature of our adventures had changed. Not only because I had *four* dogs now and only *one* me, but because time is the one thing we couldn't outrun.

Bucket's and Dagwood's faces sprouted more and more white fur as the world spun on around us. It wasn't something I noticed until other people pointed it out.

"Aww, this is an old guy," a man once said, leaning over to ever so gently pat the top of Bucket's head, as if she were made of glass.

"She's a girl," I snapped. I wanted to follow with, *And she's not old!* But I knew that on paper, on pure technicality... she was.

By the time Bucket turned fourteen, her face had gone from dark brindle, to salt and pepper, to almost completely white. It was much more obvious than Dagwood's changing face, since he'd been the color of golden hour his whole life. Regardless, the white fur that encircled their eyes made them look so much more expressive. Like they knew things that only old dogs knew.

With Bucket and Dagwood in their double digits, I was forced to slow down, to look at the idea of "an adventure" differently. Most of our days were spent doing what I had come to call "'splorin'."

It's driving down every dirt road just to see where it goes, just to pull over and stop whenever we want. It's a little topless sunbathing, a little aimless roaming, and a lot of watching the dogs run through fields of sagebrush glowing in the last light of the day.

It's crouching down over one lone, determined purple wildflower sprouting up through the center of an otherwise barren road.

It's climbing to the top of ridgelines just to see what's on the other side. It's leaning against the warm red walls, writing down the long, rambling thoughts that eventually become my books.

Sometimes it's a two-day trip into the most remote desert corners with a tent and a pocketful of magic mushrooms. Sometimes it's standing all in a line with the dogs on an overlook like a ragtag team of superheroes, or a pride of lions, pretending everything the light touches is ours... pretending we're the only ones in the world... pretending just for the sake of pretending, like I did when I was a kid.

I'd lie in the dirt in my finest dresses and cowboy boots, looking up at the shifting clouds and flocks of swirling turkey vultures. Throughout the day, the hot air rises off the sunbaked earth, creating a thermal that gently sweeps them up like gulls floating over the water. They get a bad rap, those birds, but spotting them in the sky doesn't always mean something's died.

Most of the time, they're just headed somewhere else.

homesick nomad

. . .

This leisurely, schedule-less wandering meant that the dogs could all move at their own pace, choose their own adventure, you could say.

Dagwood is famous for his morning rounds, no matter *where* we happen to wake up. He doesn't move as fast anymore, but nothing will ever keep that dog from moving far. His kind of wild lingers, even at thirteen years old.

As for Bucket, if there's a swimming hole to be found, she will be off finding it. And while she *is* a bit hard of hearing these days, I still think that most times when I call for her and she doesn't come, she's just ignoring me.

Birdie darts between sagebrush in flashes of white fur, her spotted snout dipped in desert sand. The speed with which she moves out there is astounding. The muscles on her chest and legs ripple like a racehorse's.

And then, of course, I'll see Banjo's glorious little tail swishing in the air atop some far-off rock pile on the scent of a kangaroo rat.

Oftentimes, I won't see them at all. I know they're around somewhere, but where *exactly* is up to them, not me.

I no longer felt the need to climb the hardest crack or bag the biggest peak or do anything that felt like "conquering." I didn't care if my posts went viral or not. In fact, I preferred that they didn't. I just wanted to be out there as a part of it, no different than a leaf floating along the top of a muddy creek or a lizard on sandstone, basking, eyes closed, in the sun.

Matching the slowing pace of my dogs is what taught me how

to look. How to *really* look. The simplest and smallest of things evoked an indescribable amount of joy. The dogs splashing through a puddle. A juniper tall enough to cast a shadow in the peak of the high sun. The windows down on a dirt road.

The things we forget are remarkable.

The dogs and I had spent days on end doing all of these things with dirt in our fur and light in our eyes, blissfully unaware of what day or time it was. One afternoon, as we headed toward one of our favorite petrified sand dunes, I felt Bertha's engine rev once, twice, and then fall silent as she rolled to a stop like she had so many, many times before.

All that money . . . all that effort . . . all that imagining us back out on the road . . .

I was crushed, but more importantly, I was defeated.

"I'm fucking done!" I cried into the phone to William as I paced outside a mechanic's shop in Moab.

"I can't fucking do this anymore!"

"I know, honey, I'm sorry . . ." he offered gently.

It was the angriest I'd ever been at Bertha, but he knew as well as I did that what I was saying wasn't true. Like telling your partner that you've had it and you're gonna leave your bratty, out-of-control kid at the next rest stop.

Despite how simple it would be to open the door, shove them out, and drive away, you'd never *actually* do it. Despite how simple it would be to make one Instagram post, announcing that after an entire decade of adventures and memories—after never feeling as at home *anywhere* else as I do behind the wheel of that van—that it was time to let her go.

I could probably sell her for asking cost in three minutes or less, but the idea of a stranger in my custom cow print driver's seat is enough to make me physically ill.

After all, being stubborn is what Bertha and I have always had in common.

My mother might be surprised to learn that it was advice from *her*, of all people, that has kept me so committed to Bertha all these years.

It's not that she didn't understand my love for her; she's just always seen her for what she realistically is . . . which is an old, unreliable van.

There was one breakdown many years ago (God knows where, they all blend together after a while) during which I cried to her over the phone. "It's one fucking thing after another with this van! It's like I'm playing a nonstop game of Whac-A-Mole."

"Brianna," she said to me, with a calm kind of . . . knowing . . . in her voice, "even if you were living in a house on a cul-de-sac, it would still be *one fucking thing after another*. The water heater goes out, a windstorm drops a tree branch onto the garage, the basement floods, the utility bills go up. You name it. There's always going to be *something* to figure out, whether your house has wheels or not."

Those are the words that popped into my mind every time I've threatened to give up on Bertha. Because she's right. There really is no "easy" choice, no life path that protects you from discomfort entirely. For every person lying in a van somewhere wondering what they're doing, there's a person lying in a three bedroom, two bathroom house wondering the same.

They weren't always conventional, and they certainly weren't always easy, but when all was said and done, I was still incredibly proud of my choices. Once you come to terms with the fact that there will always be things to fix, doubts to be had, mistakes to be made, you'll understand why it's so important to make your own.

After having both fuel pumps replaced, Bertha had thus far been successfully charioting us from Moab back to Bend. I had pulled over the night before to camp, just over the Oregon state line. It was a good way to break up the thirteen-hour drive . . . and a good way to squeeze in one more night asleep in that van beneath the stars.

I was leaning up against Bertha's hood, watching the dogs run through a field bathed in the light of the rising sun, when I realized that it was the mornings I missed the most.

The light creeps in slowly, the new day glowing around the edges of the burnt-orange velvet drapes. The moment William and I exchange a single word, it's followed by Birdie's thump-thump-thumping tail. *They're awake! It's happening!*

Bucket will already be standing stoically in the doorway, stomping her paws against the hardwood, outraged that breakfast has yet to be served.

From behind her, more paws. Banjo comes storming down the hallway like a sheriff in a small town, followed closely by Dagwood, whose back paws make a distinct little hop-skip sound that I'd know anywhere. He leaps up and stands over me with his ears pinned back, smiling, licking every inch of my face. I'm sure his tail would be wagging if it were still there.

Banjo army-crawls his way up William's chest, playfully snuffing and flashing his pearly teeth. Sometimes he even howls us a little tune. Birdie stays as still as possible, pressed against my side, ensuring that no one can get closer to me than her.

Then William gets up, and Bucket gets in, and I lie there with all four dogs stretched out, surrounding me, sleeping again. With my eyes still closed, I can hear William at the coffee grinder. I can smell that he's turned on the fireplace.

I sat on the roadside somewhere between Moab and Bend, grinning into my cup of instant coffee, its surface slicked with dirt and dog hair. When I closed my eyes, I could feel the warmth of William beside me in bed . . . feel the rug in the hallway beneath my feet, the chill that came in each time Banjo burst through the dog door into the backyard to check on the rat that lives in the woodpile.

I sat out in the wild in my beloved van . . . and daydreamed of my own little version of domestic bliss, of the man who was as steady as the walls of his home. The man who'd helped me keep my promise to myself, that one day I'd be rumbling down some dirt road in Bertha again.

Now, if you think I didn't up and drive right back down to Moab again a few weeks later ... you've got the wrong girl.

But on that morning, I sat there and let myself feel something I could no longer fight. Something I no longer *wanted* to fight. In a way, I had the best of both worlds. I had an equal longing for the places I'd been and the places I'd yet to go.

"I guess I just have a lot to do and a lot to miss," I said to my mother on the phone one afternoon. "I'm, like ... a homesick nomad." I laughed.

"Hmm," she mumbled, distractedly, "that would make a good book title someday."

ACKNOWLEDGMENTS

Thank you to William, for letting me turn your house into a zoo and loving all the creatures in it, including me.

To Bucket, Dagwood, Birdie, Banjo, Delilah, Bean, and Mae. None of you can read but I love you endlessly.

To my mother, for winding me up and watching me go, and for reminding me that I always was who I am. And I'm so grateful for my Wyatt, my blue-eyed boy, the only baby I'll ever have. You'd better not be reading this, you're too young, but if you are, I love you, kiddo.

Thank you to my beloved friends who lived so many of these stories alongside me, and then listened to me read the rough drafts in their backyards over gin and cigarettes.

I would be lost without my agent, Abby Saul, who knows that beneath the bestselling author is just a girl who's still worried if she's enough. No one in the world builds me up quite like you.

Thank you to my whole team at HarperOne, and my editor, Gabriella Page-Fort, with whom I share a home state and a westbound spirit.

ACKNOWLEDGMENTS

Lastly, this book delved into some of the darkest corners of social media, and for a long time I let them overshadow all the light. The reality is, there are many *more* thousands of people who've followed along, saved my dog, bought my books, hugged me on the sidewalk, told me my words meant something to them. Thank you all for reminding me why I started telling stories in the first place.

And to Selena. After everything I'd been through with anonymous people on the internet, I could never have predicted that one would save my life.

I will be endlessly grateful to you for the rest of it.

ABOUT THE AUTHOR

BRIANNA MADIA has lived a life of relentless intention, traveling the deserts of the American West in an old Ford van. She made a name for herself on social media with her inspiring captions-cum-essays about bravery, identity, nature, and subverting expectations. She splits her time between Utah and Oregon with her fiancé, two snakes, and five dogs. Her previous books, *Nowhere for Very Long* and *Never Leave the Dogs Behind*, were *New York Times* bestsellers.